Dinner at Iolani Palace.

DECEMBER 14TH, 1883.

MENU.

SOUP:

Turtle.   Mullagatawny.

FISH:

Kumu.   Crabs.   Mullet.

ENTREES:

Salmi of Duck.   Lawalud Pigeon.   Cutlets.

ROAST:

Chicken.   Beef a la mode.

Shrimp Curry.

Cheese.   Salad.

Iolani Pudding.   Jelly.   Fruit Cake.

ICE CREAM.

TEA.   COFFEE.

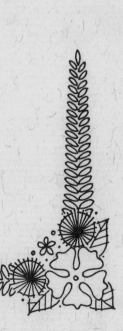

HAWAII COOKS

Metropolitan Meat Co.

Honolulu, H. I., Feb. 1st, 1893.

On and after this date our Retail Price for Meats will be as follows :

BEEF.

Loin and Porterhouse Roasts,	15 Cents per lb.
" " Steaks,	15 " "
Sirloin Steaks,	12½ " "
Round Steaks,	10 " "
Rib Roasts	10 " "
Shoulder Roasts,	8 " "
Boiling Pieces (Fresh and Corned)	10 " "

VEAL.

Loin and Fillets	15 Cents per lb.
Rib Roasts	12½ " "
Cutlets,	15 " "
Breasts,	10 " "

MUTTON.

Legs and Shoulders,	15 Cents per lb.
Loins and Ribs,	20 " "
Loin and Rib Chops,	20 " "
Shoulder Chops,	15 " "
Neck and Breast	12½ " "

The whole of the Veal and Mutton and the Ribs and Loins of Beef from this Market are refrigerated and are from two to three days old before being delivered to customers.

Bills payable weekly and monthly.

Yours respectfully,

G. J. WALLER.

Manager Met. Meat Co.

HAWAII COOKS
by
Maili Yardley

CHARLES E. TUTTLE COMPANY

Rutland, Vermont   Tokyo, Japan

REPRESENTATIVES

CONTINENTAL EUROPE
Boxerbooks, Inc.
Zurich

BRITISH ISLES
Prentice-Hall International, Inc.
London

AUSTRALASIA
Paul Flesch & Co., Pty. Ltd.
Melbourne

CANADA
M. G. Hurtig Ltd.
Edmonton

Published by the Charles E. Tuttle Company, Inc.
of Rutland, Vermont & Tokyo, Japan
with editorial offices at
2-6, Suido 1-chome, Bunkyo-ku, Tokyo, Japan, 112

Copyright in Japan, 1970, by
The Charles E. Tuttle Company, Inc.
All rights reserved
First edition 1970

Book plan by Roland A. Mulhauser
Library of Congress catalog card no. 76-104209
Standard book number 8048-0878-3

PRINTED IN JAPAN

This book is fondly dedicated to the memory of my mother, ADELINE HOSE FROST. *Her love of life, fun, family, and friends make for many endearing memories of Hawaii Nei, and her kitchen the path of many happy meals*

*Thou dost cause the grass to grow for the
    cattle,
    And plants for man to cultivate,
That he may bring forth food from the
    earth,
    And wine to gladden the heart of man,
Oil to make his face shine,
    And bread to strengthen man's heart.*
                              PSALM 104: 14 and 15

CONTENTS

Introduction, 9

Hawaiian Hospitality, 10

Basics, 16

Pupus, 17

Beverages, 22

Soups & Sandwiches, 26

Salads, 31

Fish, 37

Meats, 45

Vegetables, 61

Fruits and Preserves, 68

Desserts, 84

Miscellany, 96

Chronology, 99

Glossary, 100

Who's Who, 102

Index, 103

INTRODUCTION

AFTER MONTHS OF WORK compiling this book, I must first make a deep bow of appreciation to my husband, Paul, for his patience, time, and constructive criticism. Without his help and encouragement this might never have come to pass.

And to all my wonderful friends who were so great in giving liberally of their time and recipes to make this book possible . . . my fondest *aloha* and *mahalo*. For the most part when I asked for a recipe (which I knew they made well), there was a long pause and then, "Oh, I never measure!" So to these "by-feel-and-taste" cooks a special thanks for their "acting out" the recipes for publication. I double checked many times with the book, *Fruits of Hawaii* by Carey D. Miller, Katherine Bazore and Mary Bartow and highly recommend it for Hawaiian Kitchens.

Please bear with the 'brushes' with Hawaiiana and the reminiscences. It is my sincere hope, however, that the recipe pages of this book will be dappled with sugar, butter, catsup, soy . . . and all enjoyed for years to come—the recipes that is!

HAWAIIAN HOSPITALITY

MY DOLLS WERE THE FIRST patrons of my culinary art. At the age of six I created for them wonderful gooey concoctions by mashing petals of the double hibiscus with water until they turned to a gelatinous mess. Later came sessions of creamed tuna lumps, soggy rice, leaden biscuits and chocolate glue in the hallowed halls of Punahou School a good forty years ago. All I can say is, thank goodness the dolls could never refuse, and bless Miss Irwin for her patience in trying to show us the proper way to a man's heart.

As I look back on the Hawaii of my youth, I see a panorama of sprawling homes, wide lanais, lawns, trees, "chop suey" gardens, formal walks, arbors, masses of flowers, streams to swim in, swimming tanks, and warm hospitality that came naturally and with lots of *aloha*.

Time moved more slowly then. Our elders loved to stop and visit, whether downtown in the Liberty House, C. J. Day and Company, or the old Metropolitan Meat Market with its cages (to carry packages and bills) buzzing back and forth overhead, or in the home. Families called on families. We went for long rides, stopping along the way to visit. Kids were kids, and the beaches and mountains were all theirs for the asking. "Aunty Mary" had homemade candy, cake, or cookies any time of the day. Familiar and faithful servants would always give us the "time of day" and make us feel important. Summer spread the frosting on the cake . . . long vacations on the beaches in the country or visits to the outside islands by slow cattle boat. Hawaiian time they called it, and Hawaiian hospitality grew naturally in this atmosphere of leisurely aloha.

The outside world met Hawaiian hospitality in the late 1700's with the arrival of the first sailing ships. The natives gave lavishly of fresh pigs, fish, sweet potatoes, bananas, *taro*, yams, coconuts, breadfruit, and gourds, not to mention *awa*. This was the *hookupu*, the custom of giving the fruits of the land.

Kamehameha I, a giant among men, offered hospitality on a giant scale. His celebrations and luaus lasted for weeks.

A Spaniard, Don Francisco de Paula Marin, arrived in 1791 and introduced or cultivated many of the Island fruits, including grapes, figs, avocado, and mango. His greatest contribution to the Island hospitality was wine and beer, but his original recipes have never been found.

As frog legs and snails were delicacies of other lands, so was the dog considered choice by the Hawaiians. Like Strasbourg geese, these animals were penned and fed only the proper foods to improve the flavor . . . cooked *taro* or breadfruit mixed with coconut milk and other vegetables. Ten pounds was considered the average suckling size.

With the coming of the missionaries in 1841, the popularity of choice suckling dog was diminished and discouraged and definitely frowned upon. Those New Englanders took a dim view of many native customs and turned more to their black books and thick Fanny Farmers.

King Kalakaua was nicknamed the "Merry Monarch" and his fame as one of the greatest hosts of his time reflected his charming hospitality and trained Hawaiian entertainers. He traveled around the world and returned to the Islands with enthusiastic royal ideas.

He built Iolani Palace for his residence and following the protocol of Europe, introduced thrones, crowns, and orders to his court. Iolani Palace still stands . . . the only palace in America.

The king loved his parties, and he and the jet set of his court danced 'til dawn after dining at a sumptuous board. A different wine accompanied each of the seven or eight dinner courses. No fish 'n *poi* here. No standing over a hot *imu*! His guests dined on the likes of turtle soup, Hawaiian fish, sweetbreads, oysters, sirloin beef, fresh asparagus, turkey, pigeon pies, cheese cakes, and blanc mange, to mention a few. His china, glass, and silver were especially ordered from Europe or China, and remnants of them remain prized possessions of Islanders today. For the masses he gave *luaus* and gatherings on the Palace lawns that sometimes numbered a thousand.

The late Princess David Kawananakoa dispensed Hawaiian hospitality to friends, relatives, congressmen, royalty from foreign lands, statesmen, and other famous people. She loved to plan her parties down to the last detail. I can remember Jimmy Williams, the photographer, getting his instructions for special movies and stills of the party, the carpenters setting up the stages for the entertainment, rehearsals of the hand-picked musicians and hula dancers and the honest-to-goodness *mele* chanters, and Mary, the dear Portuguese sewing lady, polishing the brilliant tiara. Uncle Ernest Parker, a born artist and the dean of flowers, arrived the day of the party to create floral masterpieces for the tables. He was a tall, heavy-set man, but his adeptness with flowers made those large hands seem almost dainty. His use of *ti* leaf bows is still copied today.

When she entertained the Prince and Princess of Sweden, Princess Kawananakoa had the invited ladies preview their *holokus* for her approval and rehearse the proper curtsy before royalty. When she entertained the King and Queen of Siam, the scene was set from the moment they turned into her yard. Torches were placed on poles at short intervals up the long driveway leading to the lanai where she regally awaited their majesties. Handsome young Hawaiian boys in *malos* and feather capes held spears and stood at attention between the torches. She also entertained the present Duke of Windsor, then the Prince of Wales.

The days of gracious *poi* suppers and old-style home entertaining are all gone . . . *pau* now. Today the jets pour in, friends of friends of friends phone, old friends retreat to mountains, seashore and outside islands, the tempo in even the Hawaiian music is stepped up, and the snappy restaurants and the hoopla of Waikiki have taken over.

For a *poi* supper in days gone by the table decor was as important as the food. The basic requirement was fresh green *ti* leaves ribbed (center rib removed). These were placed closely down the length of each side of the table, concealing the heavy brown paper underneath. More *ti* leaves down the center hid the ends of the side leaves, and on top of this there was always either *lawai*, lacy maidenhair, *palapalai* or other mountain ferns. Flowers were used in several ways . . . strung in *leis* and swagged down the center and sides, or stuck on toothpicks to form pom-poms on tall standards, or in clusters around a *ti* leaf bow.

In most cases fresh fruit also decorated the table. Reminiscent of Colonial times, large epergnes held a variety of luscious, colorful fruit to be admired during the meal and eaten later. Or the fruit would be artfully arranged down the center of the table with watermelon sliced Van Dyke style and crowned pineapple as the focal points. Papaya, yellow and red bananas, grapes and other fruits in season filled the center of the table.

Elegantly set, the table sparkled with long stemmed crystal wine and water goblets, polished coconut dishes, crystal finger bowls with slices of lemon and flowers or geranium leaves, double damask dinner napkins, place cards, but no silverware! Always *leis* hung over each guest's chair . . . *maile* for the men and carnation, ginger, or tuberose for the ladies.

The women wore silk or brocade *holokus* with long trains. The men wore either tuxedos or white flannel pants, long sleeved white shirts (usually of fine Japanese silk) open at the neck, and red silk sashes edged with wide fringe which tied at the waist and hung at the side. The gentlemen worked at the art of wrapping these sashes several times around their waists and tying them properly . . . no semblance to the cummerbund worn today.

Hawaiians insisted that hot dishes be served piping hot and cold food cold. While the hot food steamed in the kitchen, a fruit cocktail was served first, usually in half a papaya or small pineapple with the crown intact. For this course only, you were given a spoon. Before each guest's place was a condiment or relish dish containing *kukui* nut, red salt, green onions, chili peppers, *limu*, slices of dried fish, and dried *opai* (shrimp). Stemmed coconut bowls held the one- or two-finger day-old *poi*. Crystal or coconut dishes contained *lomi lomi* salmon, fresh *opihis*, squid, and squares of *haupia* swimming in coconut cream. Scattered down the table between the guests were cooked sweet crabs (to be eaten with great aplomb and finesse) and pieces of baked banana and sweet potato.

Before the eating started, a Hawaiian gentleman from amongst the guests was asked to say the prayer. Everyone stood and bowed his head in silence while the benediction was offered, and then the feast began. While the spoons and cocktail remains were being removed, the guests started on the cold food before them and the "many hands" of the old days brought in the hot dishes. Before each guest was set a plate with a steaming hot *lau lau*, a crystal dish of pig cooked in the *imu*, coconut dishes full of chicken and *luau* with coconut cream, and tender squid in coconut cream. The different kinds of raw fish were passed, and the sweet, fat mullet baked in *ti* leaves. Champagne or wine glasses were never empty. Fingers, dainty or masculine but always graceful, dipped in the various dishes. There was lots of laughter, and appreciation of the food was evident and universal. Rarely was a guest unfamiliar with the fare, and if you didn't like a particular dish you merely turned quietly to the right or left to offer it with a smile.

Dinner time was when the music boys took over and sang merrily along, serenading individuals with their favorite songs.

The *kamaaina* had to stand while the boys played his family song. During the inevitable speeches, the musicians had their dinner, and coffee was served with fresh coconut cake, *haupia* pudding and the fresh fruit. All this feasting was never rushed but leisurely enjoyed. Later the guests adjourned to the lanai or lawn to listen to the music and watch the professional *hula* girls swish in their fresh *ti* leaf skirts and flower *leis*. Eventually the tried and true old-timers would be urged to do a *hula* to show the young how it was really done! Nothing more graceful than a pleasingly plump Hawaiian woman in her *holoku* dancing and somehow kicking her train behind her without losing a beat. If she got a man up to dance with her, he would tie his jacket around his waist and enter into the spirit of the dance.

This was the formal hospitality of my parents' days. To me as a child the essence of real down-to-earth hospitality was going to dear Bella Bisho's house on Pauoa Road (the freeway now goes through where the house stood) and finding hot bread just coming out of the oven. The Portuguese had a knack of making big, crusty, doughy-middle loaves of white bread, besides the yellow sweetbread. Who thought of calories when everyone plied you with steaming, soggy slices slathered with butter?

Bella was a family institution and beloved by us all. She worked for many *kamaaina* families ... the Cunhas, Campbells, Shingles, Tenneys, the Princess, and many others.

She worked like a trojan, talked in a raspy high-pitched voice with hands waving, took in laundry, did housework, and "baby-sat" when parents took trips. Besides raising a large family of her own and sending them all to parochial schools, she still had time to do the most exquisite embroidery and monogramming. Because she told me many years ago never to store starched linen, to this day her delicate lace cloths and napkins are carefully wrapped in blue tissue unstarched and unironed until the special occasion arises.

The mention of the names Louise and Walter Dillingham is like throwing a switch and lighting up a memorable era of Hawaii. They had a warm love and deep interest in their Hawaii. Their home, La Pietra, was the scene of many brilliant gatherings, and the guest book reads like a "Who's Who of the World," but it also was the hub of a lively family . . . one lovely daughter and three handsome sons. *Kamaainas* agree that no one has ever really taken Mrs. Dillingham's place as the premier hostess of Hawaii.

Walter Dillingham and his three sons formed a polo team which played against crack teams from Maui, against Army teams which included a hell-for-leather rider later famous as General Patton, and against high-goal teams from the mainland. Polo was played in those days in Kapiolani Park, conveniently close to La Pietra where the parties afterwards were famous.

Those of us who were around think that there has never been anything like the fun of the thirties in Hawaii! Dancing under the stars at the Royal Hawaiian Hotel and Waialae Golf Club, and the roof garden of the Alexander Young Hotel where all the young gathered. Horseback rides along the beach at Kahala on moonlight nights, beach picnics with huge bonfires, boat sailings with ginger *leis* a quarter and the inevitable tears, sailing Stars and PCs around Pearl Harbor and movies on Ford Island Saturday night.

But then Hawaiian hospitality went to war! We never suffered the hardships of food rationing . . . there was ample to eat, fresh and good. Gasoline was rationed, but somehow we could always find an extra coupon to get us through the month. But liquor was another thing. At the onset of the war the military law left us dry for a spell and then gave us ration cards for a weekly quota of either a quart of liquor, a case of beer or a gallon of wine. Gathering the weekly quota became an important event. Juggling heavy gas masks, we patiently lined up in front of the liquor department, bought our weekly ration, and then oh so carefully took it home. One local matron today still patronizes the same liquor store because she dropped her bottle after paying for it and the kind man gave her another.

Many minds and hands at work came up with various drastic recipes to stretch the grog. One formula called for bourbon, champagne, and log cabin syrup. Somehow we all survived the locally made Five Islands Gin (known affectionately as "Five

Ulcers"), home brews, and fermented pine-apple juice which stood in a crock in many a corner.

Curfew and blackouts at sundown brought evening entertaining to a grinding halt. Tea dances came into vogue and Hawaii came to know and appreciate . . . and in some cases love . . . America's armed forces. Then blackout parties started an innovation . . . B.Y.O.B., bring your own bottles. Special passes to be on the streets after curfew had to be obtained from the military; otherwise you took your chances creeping through the darkened streets and avoiding the MP. Day-time beach picnics were popular, but it was a problem to find a quiet, unfortified beach.

Many of the hospitable *kamaainas* turned their country homes over to the U.S.O. for rest and recreation for the boys. Princess Kawanankoa gave her home at Malaekahana. On Molokai Mr. and Mrs. George Cooke invited war-weary men into their home to relax for a few days. The late Chris Holmes's large home, now the "Queen's Surf," was the fly-boys' headquarters, and the Royal Hawaiian Hotel was stripped of her grandeur for the submariners.

The war ended and hospitality survived, but a new era emerged. Thousands of men had discovered the Islands while on duty here and wanted to return with their families. Hundreds of thousands of dollars were poured into advertising these paradise isles, and the Hawaii Visitor's Bureau beckoned enticingly. The result was inevitable . . . on came the curious from the mainland, and the number increases daily. Many remain and find a place in the sun.

However, through all the ages Hawaiian hospitality still retains its unique charm. The magnificent outdoors, the sun, the moonlight, the sea, year round picnics and barbecues, the formal and the informal par-ties all have an Island flavor. The different customs and foods reflect the various nation-alities who live in harmony in our beautiful Hawaiian Islands and contribute the best from their homelands.

BASICS

BEFORE WE START to pore over recipes, let's mention some of the stand-bys to be found in a Hawaiian kitchen.

One prime requisite is Hawaiian rock salt . . . *pa'a kai*. Disregard the bit about "unfit for human consumption" on the label and discover its distinctive flavor and many uses. The white salt is used strictly for cooking, and the red is used at table for seasoning. The Hawaiians have always used *pa'a kai* not only for food but for medicinal purposes.

Aloe is planted outside many a kitchen. It is positive magic for burns. Cut the leaf and quickly apply the slimy, smelly liquid to the burned area, and soon thereafter pain and redness will disappear.

Likewise mint is found growing under faucets or in pots near the kitchen.

Ginger, garlic and onion have grown since before time, and no Island home is without an ample supply. These little roots are used in the majority of Island recipes.

Punk is still used on *lanais* and outdoor areas where mosquitos are a nuisance, especially in the valleys and seashore. These green coils from the Orient have a fragrant odor, much more pleasant than the spray bomb.

You will usually find a jelly bag, for straining the fruit juice from the pulp, stashed away in a kitchen drawer. The old-fashioned pelum or netting is hard to come by today, but double thicknesses of cheese cloth work just as well and can be thrown away after using.

Somewhere there is always a grill, be it portable or an elaborate barbecue pit. Meat always tastes better cooked over charcoal. If you live in the valleys, the kind of grill that has a cover will save many a rained-out steak.

Soy sauce is usually bought by the gallon or half gallon as it is constantly being used in cooking, and many people keep a cruet of soy for the table besides the usual salt and pepper.

Many recipes call for Ajinomoto,* the Japanese version of seasoning salt. The Chinese contribution to seasoning is Chi-

Ajinomoto is actually a trade name for mono-sodium glutamate, but at least in Hawaii it is as much of a household word as Coca Cola.

nese five spices, and from India comes curry powder in various degrees of heat.

You can buy raw sugar in cellophane bags, and many prefer the light brown crystals for table use and in recipes which call for brown sugar. This is unrefined sugar milled in Hawaii.

A few cans of crushed or whole pineapple should be on the reserve shelf at all times and frozen coconut milk in the freezer.

The island of Maui grows large white onions which are noted for being juicy and sweet, and therefore preferred by most Islanders . . . raw, pickled, or in cooking.

PUPUS

COCKTAIL PARTIES ARE BIG in the Islands. Some serious-minded businessmen detest them, and it's a loyal wife who will trot dutifully home early to a spot of soup. Honolulu is an early-rising town and likewise to bed.

The usual cooktail invitation reads 6–8 p.m., but often at 6:30 the host and hostess stand looking at each other with misgivings. However, soon thereafter the action begins and gathers momentum just about eight o'clock. Most people have their favorite cateress and bartenders, who know the guests and their drinks. Social prestige in Honolulu is measured by which bartenders know what you drink without having to ask. The cateress is usually booked months in advance with the result that many a party date is set around her available time.

An elaborate cocktail party menu usually includes a wide variety of oriental dishes as well as the familiar standbys of cheese puffs, raw vegetables, and assorted nuts. *Sashimi,* sliced raw fish, is high on the popularity list. Another Japanese platter that empties before it circles the room is shrimp *tempura,* deep fried shrimp in batter. Some people make their dinner on the *teriyaki* meat sticks that are grilled outside over a small *hibachi* and served hot. A platter of fresh lobster cut in generous pieces served with a spicy sauce is very popular, especially with dieters. The Chinese dish of crisp won ton, deep fried pork ravioli, is another winner. A Hawaiian touch is added with a platter of cubed *kalua pig* with *poi* and red salt. Baby tomatoes stuffed with salt salmon and green onions is a complimentary dish. But never under estimate the public acclaim of the old standby, cream cheese and clam dip with potato chips. Somehow there is never enough!

In most cases the hostess will serve a buffet of assorted breads and cold meats, or if the *pupus* were on the light side a big pot of stew and rice will balance off the evening.

Avocado Dip

This rich mix is more for crackers than chips because of its oleo-like consistency. In an electric blender mix 2 t lemon juice; 2 t minced or grated onion; 1 or more t Worcestershire sauce; 1 C diced avocado; 1 t salt and let it whirl. When well blended, add 1 8-oz. package of softened Philadelphia cream cheese a little at a time to blend thoroughly. Chill well. This is better made the day before as it hardens as it sits.

Curry Dip with Vegetables

For an attractive and tasty platter arrange raw carrot sticks, crisp celery stalks, raw cauliflower petals, sliced green peppers, and shiny sliced red apples around a bowl of the following mix: 1 C mayonnaise; 2 hard-cooked eggs grated very fine; finely chopped green onion, the whole stalk; curry powder to taste; a 4½-oz. can of either shrimp, crab, or lobster shredded and sprinkled generously with lemon juice. Mix well and season with garlic salt, pepper, Worcester-

shire sauce or whatever your taste . . . substantial and popular.

Chutney Cheese Spread

For an easy mix, mash up home-made chutney with a small 3-oz. package of softened Philadelphia cream cheese . . . half and half . . . and add a little chutney syrup to moisten. Spread on toast rounds or crackers.

Abalone

Cut a 1-lb. can of abalone in bite-size pieces and put in serving bowl with some of the liquid. Serve with a jigger full of tooth picks and either plain soy or the soy mustard sauce. Simple and good.

Basic Soy Sauce

In a small bowl mix 1 T hot powdered mustard slowly with 1 t water for a paste and then slowly add 2 T soy sauce, or until desired taste and consistency. Optional: dash of aji, t. of sesame oil or a small amount of grated fresh ginger.

Kalua Pig Platter

In the meat chapter are details for cooking *kalua* pig. For *pupus* cook the roast the day before, cut the cold pork in bite-size chunks next day and warm for serving. Place on platter covered with green *ti* leaf, and add cubes of cooked *taro*. A jigger of red salt for those who like it saltier and another jigger of toothpicks for easy eating. You may use plain poi instead of the *taro*.

Cherry Tomatoes and Salmon

Soak one pound of salt salmon for at least three hours or until not too salty . . . change water frequently. Shred meat from skin and bones and combine with six diced, peeled tomatoes and several stalks of green onions sliced very thin. Clean cherry tomatoes, cut off tops, scoop out meat and add to salmon, then stuff the mixture back into shell. This goes well with the pig platter.

Sashimi

The secret of good *sashimi* lies in the choice of fresh fish. You can use any big fish . . . tuna, *ahi*, swordfish or *ulua*. If you have a friendly fish man he may slice it in serving pieces for you, otherwise use a very sharp knife (there are special *sashimi* knives). Remove the skin, slice the fillet diagonally in thin slices trying to overlap each piece as you cut so you can pick it all up with the knife to lay on a platter of shredded lettuce

or cabbage. Serve cold with separate dish of hot soy sauce.

Teriyaki Sticks

For about twenty people you need two pounds of good beef sirloin tip. Maybe the nice butcher will cut it in thin strips for you . . . otherwise with a sharp knife slice meat 1¼″ wide by 1″ long and ¼″ thick. Soak the sliced meat for about an hour or longer in a sauce of 3 C soy; ½ C brown sugar; clove of garlic sliced thin, and finger of peeled, crushed ginger. Spot of gin or bourbon optional but sure to improve flavor! If you are having a cateress, let her fix the sticks as she will have the knack of threading the meat on the small bamboo sticks. Cook the meat sticks quickly over a low charcoal fire and serve immediately. To keep bamboo from burning, soak sticks in water before using.

Crisp Won Ton

You may buy crisp won ton at the chop suey house, but once you learn the art of making and wrapping them you can form an assembly line and literally make hundreds in no time. For about 45 buy 1 10-oz. package of *won ton pi* (moist) wrappers . . . most grocery stores carry this. Fry ¾ lb. ground pork until cooked, add 3 large minced shrimp, ½ 12-oz. can chopped luncheon meat, 4 chopped water chestnuts, 4 stalks chopped green onion, 1 unbeaten egg, 1 T soy, 1 t salt, aji, and 1 t sugar. When mixture is cool, drop 1 t of filling on square, moisten edge of wrapper with water and press firmly together into triangles or rectangles. Deep fry in hot oil, turning once, until brown, drain on paper towel, and serve hot. These can be prepared in advance, frozen and deep fried when needed.

Tahitian Raw Fish

White fish is preferable, but again any big fresh fish will do. Cut in small pieces and mix with rock salt and allow to stand for 2–3 hours or until the salt has completely permeated the fish. Rinse, leaving some salt and then cover the fish completely with lots of fresh LIME juice . . . don't spare the lime juice as this is the important step in 'cooking' the fish. Cover and leave overnight in refrigerator. Next day pour off the lime juice, cover with coconut cream and add shredded carrots, thinly sliced onions and slivered celery hearts . . . mix well and serve very cold and watch it disappear!

Shrimp Tempura

Prepare two pounds of raw shrimps but leave the tails for "handles". Dip the whole shrimp in batter, drop quickly into deep hot

fat until browned and turn once. Place on paper towel to absorb grease and serve with soy sauce dip. Batter: Mix together 2 eggs, ½ C flour, ½ C cornstarch, ½ t salt, and ¾ to 1 C soup stock.

Stuffed Lychees

Add chopped macadamia nuts to softened Philadelphia cream cheese and form into small balls to stuff in seed hole of canned lychees.

Macadamia Nuts

To double the flavor, roast nuts in slow oven to brown slightly and serve hot.

Peanuts

Add a dash of curry powder to peanuts and warm in oven.

DORA (MRS. STEPHEN) DERBY calls this one. . . .

Hawaiian Fish Around

Put a cup or more of Miracle Whip (has to be this) in double boiler and season to taste. Add drained button mushrooms, pickled pearl onions, sweet gerkins, cocktail sausages or Vienna sausages cut in quarters, or anything else in the meat line but don't try mixing sea food with this. Serve with tooth picks and the guests just fish around!

Through the kindness of Mr. Ben F. Dillingham we are able to use several recipes of his mother, the late Mrs. Walter F. Dillingham, which she served at La Pietra over the years.

Chutney Toast Rounds

Toast bread on one side and cut in rounds. Butter and spread untoasted side with chutney. Sprinkle grated nippy cheese over top and put under broiler until cheese melts. Serve hot.

Stuffed Eggs

Cut 4 hard-cooked eggs in half lengthwise. Force yolks through sieve and add: 1 t prepared mustard, ¼ t salt, dash pepper and ½ t curry powder, 2 T mayonnaise. Blend well and refill egg whites. Sprinkle with paprika and serve garnished with ripe olives heated in their own liquid.

Shada (Mrs. Ed) Bryan adds shredded Portuguese sausage to her *taro* cakes and serves them for *pupus*. (See recipe on page 62.)

Bacon Cream Cheese

Miss Healani Lloyd says this is a do-ahead to be served with crisp toast or crackers.

Soften a large 8-oz. package of Philadelphia cream cheese, fry 8 slices of bacon very dry and crisp, and crumble. Chop 2-oz. jar green olives stuffed with pimento. Mix all together, put in serving bowl and refrigerate overnight, garnish with sliced olives and sprinkle with paprika.

Breadfruit Chips

Cleo (Mrs. Robert) Evans had an exceptionally good breadfruit tree in her front yard, and with lots of experimenting came up with this recipe.

Pick mature but not ripe breadfruit, peel, cut in sections, simmer in salted water until barely fork tender. Drain, remove core, slice very thin in large pieces, place on buttered baking sheet, sprinkle with salt, brush with melted butter and bake in 400 F oven until crisp and golden. "They just disappear," says Cleo.

Marinated Purple Onions

Muriel (Mrs. Walter E.) Flanders sent this along with the note . . . "This recipe was a wedding present."

2½ lbs. purple onions, peeled and sliced, ½ qt. cider vinegar, 1¼ cups brown sugar, 1 handful whole cloves. Marinate overnight and serve with slices of French bread. Elegant and no other *pupus* needed!

Lotus Root Pupu

PEGGY MAY (MRS. ROBERT) HUNTER made this up one day to serve to some of her *malihini* friends.

Buy firm root, peel and boil in sections for barely 10 min. Slice ⅛″ thick, fry quickly in peanut oil, and drain on absorbant paper. (Do not overcook.) When all the slices are fried, add ¼ C soy to pan and sugar to taste, simmer, (grated ginger optional), add Tabasco or chopped red chili pepper according to how hot you dare. Chill and serve very cold with tooth picks.

BEVERAGES

I'M NOT ABOVE REMEMBERING the days of the bootlegger in Hawaii! The "mystery man" quietly arrived after dark, drove up to the rear door and deposited kegs of *okolehao*. The *oke* sat (or rolled around in a rumble seat) in charcoal-lined wooden kegs until properly aged and then was siphoned into gallon bottles. That siphoning process must have been great sport in the old days . . . you just had to "suck 'em up." Depending on your supplier, *oke* sold for $5.00 to $8.00 a gallon. The story goes that *okolehao* was originally distilled in the "pot with the iron bottom" and *okolehao* literally means iron bottom!

Today if you are fortunate enough to be treated to some of the rare pre-war *oke*, you will agree that it is sheer nectar and should be savored straight like a liqueur.

One of the popular drinks for a large gathering in the thirties and forties was called "Scorpions." It is appropriately named, as like the insect it has quite a "sting." On one occasion the last minute ingredient, ginger ale, was forgotten in the mad scramble to sample the brew, and even the strongest fell.

Scorpions

Put into large crock: juice of 1 doz. oranges and 1 doz. lemons. Add 1 qt. bourbon (or *oke*) and a syrup made by boiling 1 C sugar and ¾ C water; dash of angostura and orange bitters; chopped bunch of mint (½ C), and let this stand for 24–48 hours. You MUST refrain from sampling. When ready to fire . . . add 3 qts. of ginger ale or 3 qts. sparkling soda and lots of ice . . . don't forget!

Suicide

Another one of those "party mixers." You need a big crock to hold chopped up skins and all of 3 oranges and 4 lemons. Add 1 or 2 chopped vanilla beans and 1 C sugar. Pour over all this one gallon of *"oke,"* set in cool place, securely lock and stand by for 30 days. When drained of will power and consumed with curiosity, relax and try it. Strain liquid into decanters and serve mixed with hot, strong coffee, brandy, or even try it "as is."

Kuu Home Kalua

Today this little recipe is quite popular for various reasons. Bring to boil 3½ C sugar, 2½ C water and 1 C powdered instant coffee. Let cool. Add 2 C 100 proof vodka and 1 vanilla bean cut in 4's, store in gallon bottle and let stand for 30 days. (Good time to take a trip). Discard vanilla bean and pour into decanters. It is well worth the waiting, but you must use 100 proof vodka! Some substitute bourbon. Try it over vanilla ice cream.

Mai Tai

Who doesn't envision the ocean, palm trees and amour with this exotic drink? Use giant old-fashion glasses (flower pots we called them) and fill with cracked ice. Place cherry and slice of fresh pineapple on toothpick and use for garnish. Pour into glass 1½ oz. light rum; 1½ oz. gold rum; 1 oz. Orgeat syrup; ½ oz. (or splash of) 150 proof rum on top and float on! If you're not too thirsty toss in a vanda orchid and sprig of mint. Slowly sip through straws.

Daquiri

This is a favorite cocktail at luncheon parties. The recipe is easy to remember and follow and can be made up the night before. 1 part fresh lemon or lime juice, 2 parts water and 3 parts rum. Sweeten to taste before adding liquor so sugar will dissolve. Serve over crushed or cracked ice in old-fashion glasses. One variation is to add mashed bananas and give it a whirl in the blender.

Miscellaneous

Here's another of those prohibition numbers that is left sealed and shaken occasionally for about three months. To ¾ gallon *"oke"* add 2 uncut lemons, 1 uncut orange, 1 vanilla bean and 2 lbs. sugar. I presume it takes three months for the sugar to dissolve, as this is the test of when it is ready.

* * * * *

This old tattered recipe doesn't state whether it's per glass or per round, so I leave it to your decision. Juice of 1 lemon, 4 T unsweetened grape fruit juice, 1½ jiggers grenadine, 5 jiggers of rum. Decorate with mint leaves and, I should think, lots of cracked ice!

* * * * *

Ever tried the milk of the young coconut mixed with gin?

* * * * *

Today sake, the Japanese rice wine, is being promoted into greater popularity. They say a sake martini is something else again, but the old song goes . . . "hot sake and dynamite, down in Nagasaki . . ."

* * * * *

Okolehao is being made legally and commercially today, and some contend that it does not leave a hangover.

Iced Tea

This is tops for any time of the day. Always a good idea to have those packages of instant iced tea mix, but jars of the basic in the refrigerator are always hospitable and thirst-quenching. Bring 3 qts. water to boil; add ½ C tea; 1½ C sugar and several sprigs of mint. Steep for 5 minutes and strain off tea leaves and mint; add juice of 4 lemons **WHEN COOL** . . . otherwise you have milky iced tea.

Poi Cocktail

You don't hear too much about this nourishing drink any more. A pity, too, because it is one of the best foods for invalids, children or non-eaters. Shake well 1 C milk; pinch of salt; cracked ice and 3 or 4 heaping T *poi*. Serve cold in glasses.

Coffee

Don Paulo Marin brought the first coffee beans to Hawaii in 1817. Today coffee grows in abundance around Kealakekua Bay and the upper regions of Kona and thrives on the volcanic and often rocky soil. The school year is geared to the coffee harvest so the youngsters can help pick the beans in the fall. Kona coffee is highly esteemed for its rich flavor.

Iced Coffee

Pour strong cold coffee into large container and add scoops of vanilla or coffee ice cream.

Party Fruit Punch

Make syrup of 2 C sugar and 1 C water boiled together one minute. Mix 1 C strong tea, syrup, juice of 3 oranges and 3 lemons, ½ C chopped fresh mint, 1 8¼-oz. can shredded pineapple, and let stand one hour. Pour over block of ice in punch bowl, add 1 qt. white grapefruit juice, sliced oranges and strawberries, and 4 28–oz. bottles of ginger ale. During the serving you may add sparkling water to keep it charged.

Punch

Miss Healani Lloyd uses her simple basic punch recipe for large gatherings at the Daughters of Hawaii. She did say that for other occasions it would mix well with either gin or bourbon.

1 46-oz. can pineapple juice, 28-oz. bottle ginger ale, qt. pineapple sherbet, and sprigs of mint. Or, 1 46-oz. can guava juice (she prefers the frozen concentrate), 28-oz. bottle of sparkling water, 1 quart lime sherbet and sprigs of mint . . . cool color and refreshing.

Iced Tea

Mrs. Richard A. Cooke, Sr. was one of Hawaii's beloved kamaaina hostesses and an invitation to dine with her was a privilege. I still have her pink note paper with her recipe for iced tea.

Make syrup of 2 C sugar and 1 pt. water. Pour 2½ qts. boiling water over ½ C tea and let stand for 3 minutes. Strain tea; add syrup and 4 sprigs of mint. AFTER IT COOLS add juice of 5 lemons.

Eggnog

(3 qts. or 26 small glasses)

Mrs. Sherwood Lowrey used to take this eggnog to her convalescent friends for strength and good cheer. Her mother, Mrs. Ernest Kopke, was known as a great cook and taught her five daughters the fine points of cooking so that a familiar phrase in Hawaii was "The Kopke girls' cooking."

9 eggs, separated; 2 T sugar; 1 qt. milk; 1 pt. heavy cream; 1 C brandy, ½ C rum and nutmeg to garnish. Beat egg yolks very hard then add sugar and beat well again. Add liquor slowly, then the cream and milk. Let this stand in the icebox for 2 days stirring twice daily. Before serving add stiffly beaten egg whites and 2 T or more of any sweet red wine. (Keep egg whites refrigerated until time to use.)

SOUPS & SANDWICHES

TODAY NOT MANY HOMES adhere to the old strict rule of serving soup . . . always, religiously . . . as the first course. Nor do many homes have a pot of soup simmering on the back of the stove. In the olden days the frugal housewife fed her whole family an evening meal from a pot which simmered all day with leftovers . . . meat bones, vegetables and macaroni or potato or both.

Today bouillon cups and saucers are pushed to the rear of the shelf and the old-fashioned deep soup bowls (placed on a serving plate) are seldom used.

Soup today is a treat! Real homemade soups take time but are gratefully devoured.

With everyone so calorie-conscious, sandwiches have begun to slip in popularity. However, as long as there are those brown bags and tin lunch boxes to fill and a spot of tea occasionally there will always be a sandwich!

Jook or Chook

Chinese rice gruel made the *haole* way . . . a meal in itself, delicious and good. Place a turkey carcass (or chicken) in large pot and cover with water. Worth adding Island pork bone for flavor too. Into the pot slice 2 round onions and several slices of ginger, and let this bubble and boil hard and fast for about a half hour. Then add your raw rice which has been soaking in water with sprinkle of Hawaiian rock salt (1 C rice to 7 C stock). Simmer this for several hours, but watch and stir as rice has tendency to stick to bottom of pot. When cooked down it should be the consistency of thick gruel. Remove all bones and season to taste with salt and pepper (aji optional). Ladle into Chinese soup bowls and garnish with Chinese parsley, sliced red pork, shredded lettuce and chopped green onions. Freeze the left-overs in plastic cartons.

Fish Chowder

Buy the head, bones and a little extra meat of a good Island fish. Rinse, put in pot, sprinkle with Hawaiian salt and cover with water. Simmer gently for about ten to fifteen minutes, but do not overcook the meat. Remove bones and meat from water, debone, and return bones to the stock and simmer for about 45 minutes. Set meat aside. In another pot fry up several strips of sliced bacon, add a chopped onion, and cook until done. Add the fish stock which you have, naturally, carefully strained. Bring to a boil and then add one big grated potato to thicken. Keep stirring so it won't stick and when potato is well done and stock thickened, add can cream, milk, or half and half so that it more than half balances out the stock. Season to taste and add a little rosemary, dill and basil. Now add the bits of fish and keep warm. You may sprinkle chopped parsley when serving. This with saloon pilots is a meal in itself, and is most suitable to serve in big mugs after the cocktail party has thinned out.

Hawaiian Fish Soup

I vaguely remembered my grandmother making the most delectable soup with a whole mullet, and after much inquiring found a reasonable facsimile of her recipe. Clean and scale a small fresh mullet, score it several times to the bone on either side, sprinkle with Hawaiian salt, and more than cover with water. Bring to a gentle boil and simmer to cook the fish through . . . about ten minutes. Do not overcook or it will be tough. Remove the fish to cut into serving pieces, pour the soup into bowls and add the meat. For garnish use either green onions or chopped watercress. This was always accompanied by small red chili peppers and sour poi and relished to the last bone. Lucky the one who got the head and tail!

Miso Soup

Once in a while this soup just "hits the spot," and this variation is easy and quick . . . as long as you have a tub of miso and blocks of tofu. To ½ C dried shrimps and meaty pork bone add 8 C water and simmer until pork is done. Scoop out the shrimps and bones and add 1 C miso to the boiling stock. Let this come to a rolling boil and add 2 blocks cubed tofu, pinch of salt, 1 t aji and let cook another 5 minutes. Add green onions chopped fine when ready to serve.

Oxtail Soup A la B

To 3 lbs. of oxtail add 6 pitted red dates, about 6 dried mushrooms, small pieces of orange peel, (all found in Oriental dept. of market) ½ lb. raw shelled peanuts and 6 qts. water. If you prefer, brown the meat first and then add other ingredients and seasoning. Cook several hours to boil down, refrigerate overnight, skim off fat, and cook for another few hours. A jigger or two of bourbon peps up the peanuts! Season again to taste. Serve very hot.

Pake Soup

Place 2 lbs. pork; 1 clove garlic; 1 piece ginger, crushed, in pot and cover with water. Boil for 1 hour or until pork is tender. Salt to taste. Remove pork and slice. Skim grease from liquid, add juice of 1-lb. can of abalone, bring to boil, and add 1 bunch (about 3 stalks) chopped mustard cabbage, sliced abalone and pork. Season to taste.

Cold Avocado Soup

Put in blender: 1 10½-oz. can consomme, 1 mashed avocado, juice of lemon and grated onion. When well blended fold in a little more than ½ pt. sour cream and season with salt and pepper. Chill and serve very cold.

From the Sandwich Islands

Canned corned beef is a great favorite in the Islands. Some like it from the can with poi and onions and others like it in sandwiches. To one 12-oz. can of corned beef add ½ T pickle relish, aji or favorite spice, and mayonnaise, catsup, and mustard to spreading consistency. Mash and mix well. If you all agree, add chopped onions. Good on any color bread.

* * * * *

If you really don't care about poundage . . . spread mayonnaise mixed with salt and pepper and lemon juice over 2 slices of bread, add generous slices of avocado, dribble more mayonnaise, add several pieces of dry lettuce and slap together.

* * * * *

Likewise on weight . . . mash ripe banana with peanut butter and spread between mayonnaised slices of bread. Actually, the protein value is very high.

* * * * *

When making plain tuna mix, add a little chopped celery and parsley . . . the finer the better . . . and a dash of dill seed, and a squirt of lemon.

Fish Chowder

Cut ½-lb. slices of pork in pieces and fry crisp. Add 1 T finely chopped onion and 2 C of water in which backbone and head of mullet have been boiled. Add a cup of cubed raw potatoes and cook 10 minutes. Remove meat from bones, add and simmer 10 minutes. Heat 1 C rich cream, 1 C milk, pour in and thicken with a little flour and water. Salt to taste. Serve with soda crackers crisped in the oven. From the favorite recipes of MRS. WALTER F. DILLINGHAM.

Chilled Beet Soup

MARTHA (MRS. J. ROBERT) JUDD sets a beautiful formal dinner table, and she usually serves this soup as a first course.

Drain one #303 can of beets, put in blender with one 10½-oz. can of consomme and turn to low. Add ¼ C vinegar (or less depending on taste), ¼ t salt and pepper. When well blended, refrigerate and chill well. Serve in chilled bouillon cups. Top the soup with a tablespoon of sour cream and a dab of caviar.

Cream of Spinach Soup

CATHARINE (MRS. REGINALD H.) CARTER lives in cool Nuuanu valley and soup is a popular luncheon dish in her lovely home.

Cook 1 bunch of spinach, drain and cool. Chop one round onion fine and put with spinach into blender. Add 1 13-oz. can evaporated milk and blend. Add one can water and strain. Put in double boiler and add 1 T butter, salt and pepper and t garlic puree. Serve hot. You may substitute 2 C milk or more (if thinner soup is desired) for the canned milk.

Fish Chowder

2 big potatoes (soak ½ day) diced; 5 big onions, cut small; 2½ lbs. fish . . . split, fillet and fry a little in butter . . . and boil the bones etc., strain and reserve. Make a cream sauce: Paste of 1 T butter, 1½ T flour, and add 3 C of warm milk gradually. Fry ⅓ C cubed salt pork with 2 strips of bacon, add onions, potatoes, and fish stock. Cover and cook until potatoes are done. Cut fish in small pieces and add, stir and add warm cream sauce. Cook 25–30 minutes in double boiler.

Cream of Corn Soup

Put 1 #303 can of yellow cream corn in blender with 1 C milk. Sieve with another cup of milk through strainer, add 1 T butter, salt and pepper to taste and heat in double boiler.

Split Pea Soup

ALICE (MRS. LESTER) GAMBLE usually goes to their beach house on week-ends and a big pot of soup is always good to have sitting on the back of the stove.

Soak a 1-lb. package of split green peas in water overnight. Next day wash and add to 9 C water and 1 package of ham hocks (about 3 to a pkg.). Cook with 1 stalk chopped celery, 1 large chopped onion, 1 thinly sliced carrot, 4 peppercorns, aji and salt. Cook slowly for 3–4 hours stirring occasionally. You may eat immediately, but it is better to refrigerate (it thickens) and heat again to serve.

Onion Soup

JACK (MR. JOHN C.) WALKER is true to his Maui onions. This recipe has been in the family for years.

Peel and slice 2 very large Maui onions and fry in butter in large sauce pan until very brown. Add 3 C milk, salt and pepper and 1 T cream, if desired. Hard cook 6 eggs and separate whites and yolks. Strain onions from hot stock. 20 minutes before serving sieve yolks of egg into soup to thicken. Chop egg whites into individual soup bowls and then add steaming soup.

Mulligatawny Soup

The late MRS. CLIFFORD H. KIMBALL used her sister "Mame" Forster's famous mulligatawny soup recipe as a basis for one of the delicious soups served at the Halekulani when the family owned and operated the hotel.

1 qt. chicken or veal stock, 1 large onion, 1 T butter, 1 T bacon cut up, 3 T flour, 1 T curry powder, ½ lemon, herbs to taste, 1 carrot and salt and pepper. Melt butter in soup kettle and fry bacon in it for a few minutes. Prepare vegetables by peeling and slicing, then fry. Shake in flour and curry, and fry together for few minutes. Add stock slowly, then the herbs and salt and pepper. Boil for 1 hour. Put through sieve while hot, squeeze in lemon juice and serve hot with rice.

Waiohai Iced Avocado Soup

BOB CHANG was the chef at the Halekulani for many years and then went to Waiohai Hotel with the Kimballs and there he made this soup a very popular item on the menu.

(6 Servings)

In a blender puree one large ripe avocado and 1 round onion (sliced) until well blended and smooth. Add 1 qt. half and half slowly, 2 T sherry wine, 1 T aji, salt to taste, and a dash of tabasco sauce for that zing! Strain and chill. Serve very cold in iced bowls.

Ginger Sandwiches

Bring 1 8-oz. pkg. Philadelphia cream cheese to room temperature and add ¾ of a 7-oz. jar of Chinese preserved ginger in syrup, finely chopped. Add the syrup to moisten and flavor. Spread on fresh buttered bread. "That's it . . . simple," says "BABY MAY" (MRS. ALEXANDER) ROSS.

MISS HEALANI LLOYD wound up her teaching career, joined the Daughters of Hawaii and promptly was made refreshment chairman . . . DPI's loss and the Daughters' gain! Here are several of her sandwich recipes.

Cucumber Open-face Sandwich

Buy a good brown bread, rye preferably, and cut in rounds. Clean and score a firm cucumber leaving the green skin for color, and core to remove seeds. Place cuke slices on bread and fill hole with mixture of softened cream cheese and chopped green olives. Garnish with sprigs of parsley and a bit of paprika.

Chutney and Bacon Filling

Fry 3 strips bacon crisp, crumble and add to ½ C slightly chopped mango chutney. Keep to spreading consistency . . . best on brown bread.

Chicken Filling

Combine chopped chicken, chopped red apples with skin, small raisins and slivered celery with mayonnaise to spread.

Shrimp Fill

Mash cooked shrimp with celery and cream cheese and pimento with a tiny bit of mayonnaise to moisten.

* * * * *

Healani Lloyd adds chopped macadamia nuts to cream cheese and chopped preserved ginger, and spreads on canned date nut roll. (Only for tea, please!)

* * * * *

She uses up last night's mahimahi and tartar sauce in a hearty sandwich with lettuce.

* * * * *

For a family sandwich try chopping up canned luncheon meat and mix with hamburger relish and mayonnaise to spreading consistency.

SALADS

BECAUSE OF THE IDEAL year-round climate in Hawaii, picnics and camping are popular. Hordes of people flock to beaches on week-ends and even during the week. There are many public parks with excellent facilities where one can pitch a tent, flap or lean-to . . . if you get there first! A familiar sight on broad rural beaches are fishing poles stuck in the sand, and nearby the fishermen's families huddled away from the sun gorging on picnic fare.

Luncheons in the home have been simplified due to the shortage of help. Lunch is often an aspic salad, fresh Island fruits, seafood or fowl salad . . . all of which can be prepared in advance leaving the hostess free to enjoy her guests or cards.

Hawaiian fruits in season are delicious and

a natural for salads in many combinations. Slit a pineapple (crown and all) in half, scoop out most of the flesh . . . being careful to cut in edible portions . . . and fill with your favorite fruit. For a more elaborate (and time consuming) 'bowl' use a large long watermelon cut in half lengthwise. Remove rest of pulp leaving shell of white and green rind. You may cut the rind in spikes to make it fancier. Fill with any mixture of native fruits . . . papaya, pineapple, banana, lychee, the watermelon balls and top with scoops of guava and orange sherbet at the last minute. Halved avocados make a perfect 'dish' for seafood or chicken salad.

Potato Salad

Cook six salad potatoes (large) until tender, just right: not so soft as to be mushy, and not hard. Boil six eggs in the pot at this time, too, but remove after ½ hour when hard cooked. Peel and cut up the potatoes while still hot. Start the salad the day before so the potatoes can marinate in salt and pepper, aji, dill seed, celery seed and just enough salad oil and vinegar or pickle juice to coat the potatoes. Refrigerate overnight, and the next day add 3 or 4 de-stringed stalks of celery thinly sliced, grated carrot for coloring, the chopped hard-cooked eggs, lots of finely chopped parsley, and chopped onions if you dare. The potatoes tend to soak up the

mayonnaise so be generous when adding and mix thoroughly. Add more seasoning to taste.

This is the basis of many variations. You can halve the potatoes with elbow salad macaroni. Add a can of tuna, lobster, or crab. For more color add can or frozen peas and sliced whole radishes. Pineapple chunks (#211 can) make a flavor change. Broken bits of crisp bacon and some of the drippings add greatly to the flavor. When you take potato salad on a picnic, be sure to keep it cold at all times.

Cole Slaw

Cole slaw goes with many different things, especially sandwiches or cold cuts, and even fried fish. Select a firm cabbage, wash, core and quarter, place in large wooden bowl and chop, chop, chop into minute pieces. Mix with dressing of mayonnaise, dill seed, Worcestershire sauce, salt and pepper, mustard, pickle juice and a little sugar . . . amount depending on size of cabbage and taste. For variety and crunch add chopped celery and apples, celery and crushed pineapple, celery and chopped cucumber, or even bits of marshmallow and nuts.

The Chinese vegetable, *won buck*, makes an excellent cole slaw type salad. Wash leaves thoroughly and repack, shred very thin and crispen with ice and water, drain well and toss with your favorite dressing. It is crunchy and flavorful.

Namasu or Japanese Cucumber Salad

Partly peel 1 large cucumber, leaving strips of green, and slice very thin. Sprinkle with 1 T Hawaiian salt and let stand for at least half an hour. Squeeze off excess liquid and salt. Add to mixture of 1 t mashed ginger, 2 T white sugar, ½ C vinegar and dash of aji. To perk it up add thin strips of canned abalone. By then this and hot rice constitutes a hearty meal!

Turkey Salad

For that "girlie" luncheon serve a hearty salad of cubed cold turkey, lots of slivered celery and fresh seedless grapes mixed well with mayonnaise and salt and pepper. Or try diced cantaloupe instead of the grapes. This on a large platter of crisp green lettuce surrounded by stuffed curried eggs, canned baby beets, asparagus spears, crisp watercress, and cubed tomatoes is all you need. Cold Chinese peas may be added to the platter, too, but should be strung well, parboiled and marinated in a vinegary French dressing. Warm banana bread is excellent with this.

Banana Salad

Halve bananas, place on crisp lettuce leaves and top with mayonnaise, chopped nuts (walnuts, peanuts or macadamia) and a cherry.

Stuffed Avocado

Halve avocado and prick about three times with fork and fill with vinegar and pieces of slivered garlic. Let stand for ½ hour. Make a rich cream sauce . . . add crab, chicken or lobster . . . empty avocado and fill with cream mixture. Sprinkle parmesan cheese over top and put in oven to warm and brown.

Pineapple Salad

Cream together ½ C cream cheese and ¼ C mayonnaise. Beat until stiff 1 pt. whipping cream and mix thoroughly with creamed mixture, ½ C marshmallows cut fine and 1 8¼-oz. can crushed pineapple. Refrigerate for at least three hours and serve with maraschino cherries for decor.

Pineapple Gelatin Salad

Dissolve 1 pkg. lemon jello in 1 scant C of hot water and 1 C pineapple juice, add 1 T vinegar and 1 t salt. When partly set add 1 C grated carrots, 1 C drained sliced or crushed pineapple, ½ C nuts chopped fine. Serve with cottage cheese or mayonnaise.

Miscellaneous

A perky combination salad is diced avocado, sections of the ripe pomelo, and shredded lettuce. Douse with your favorite French dressing and serve very cold.

* * * * *

Fresh lychees peeled and seeded are superb in any combination of fruit salad. If not in season canned lychees will suffice.

* * * * *

I leave this for you to figure out if it is salad or dessert! Fill halved avocados with rum and powdered sugar!!!

Unusual French Dressing

2 parts olive oil to 1 part lemon juice or vinegar and instead of salt, crush 1 large anchovy and shake well. Pour over crisp lettuce in large bowl which has been rubbed with garlic.

Cucumber-Pineapple Salad

"Sis" (Mrs. Ross) Sutherland is the salad maker of the Shingle family!

Chop or grate 2 cukes, add 1 8¼-oz. can drained crushed pineapple, and add to 2 packages lemon jello dissolved in scant 4 C boiling water. Set to harden in refrigerator and serve on lettuce with mayonnaise.

Mango Salad

Combine small slices of Pirie mangoes with crisp, clean sprigs of watercress in large bowl and toss with your favorite dressing.

Dressing

Mix thoroughly ½ C sugar, 1 t salt, ½ t pepper, ¾ t dry mustard, and add 1 C Wesson oil, ½ C vinegar, ½ C tomato catsup, and 1 grated large onion. Beat with egg beater and bottle. Keeps well in refrigerator for a long time.

Dressing For Avocado Salad

Mrs. Frank Thompson is very particular about the preparation and serving of foods and is noted for her gracious tables. This is one of her favorite salads, and she says it should be a first course and served very hot.

Heat (not cook) 2 T vinegar, 2 T catsup, 2 T powdered sugar, 2 T butter, 2 T Worcestershire sauce. Stir well while heating and pour over one half of peeled avocado (per person) with seed hole down, on bed of lettuce.

Tomato Aspic Salad

Leinani (Mrs. E. B.) Peterson is a hostess noted for her old-time Hawaiian hospitality and superior food. This aspic is one of her favorite luncheon dishes.

In a pot put 2 28-oz. cans of solid "pac" tomatoes; 1 sliced stalk celery; 1 whole onion, sliced; salt and pepper; 2 cloves; 1 bay leaf, whole. Boil all together and stir so tomatoes won't stick. Add one 15-oz. can Spanish sauce and 1 C tomato juice and bring to boil. Remove bay leaf and put through strainer or ricer for the juice.

In a deep bowl soak 3½ packages gelatin with 1 C tomato juice and juice of half a lemon. When dissolved add hot liquid and stir thoroughly and cool. Pour into lightly buttered mold (rinsed in cold water) when cool so butter won't melt. This fills two 4-C molds.

Arrange the mold on a bed of green, crisp lettuce, fill the center with seafood salad (fresh lobster or crab, or a mixture of shrimp and lobster mixed with mayonnaise thinned with fresh lemon juice and seasoning to taste). Surround with deviled eggs and sliced avocado.

Potato Salad

Mrs. Peterson's mother, Mrs. Charles (Ann) Chillingsworth is well remembered as a beloved *kamaaina*. Her daughter learned the fine points of entertaining from this charming person. On Christmas Eve after church, or New Year's Eve, Mrs. Chillingsworth served a buffet at midnight. The potato salad was her specialty.

In a large pot boil 4 large unpeeled potatoes (old thin dark skinned potatoes are best) until cooked but not soft or broken. A 2-pronged fork is best for testing. They should be firm when cooked. While still hot peel potatoes, cut lengthwise and in half or thirds and slice. Sprinkle lightly with salt and pepper and cider vinegar. Use 2 dinner forks to toss. Refrigerate overnight.

Next day add 4 stalks celery, slit and sliced very thin; 4 green onions, cut off roots and peel past slimy skin and slice sliver fine with only a little of the green for color; add 1 bunch of parsley (¼–½ C) which has been rinsed, thoroughly dried and chopped fine. Toss all lightly with enough mayonnaise which has been thinned with lemon juice to coat all potato pieces. Last of all add 3 or 4 sliced hard-cooked eggs and remove to serving dish. Top salad with slices of 2 boiled eggs and sprinkle with paprika. Surround with crisp lettuce.

Original recipe called for a particular brand of dry pack shrimps sprinkled lightly through salad . . . but unfortunately they are unavailable now. Neither wet pack fresh or oriental dried can be substituted. The closest substitute is shrimps dried in shell, peeled and broken into salad.

Tomatoes and Onions with Vinaigrette Dressing

Martha (Mrs. J. Robert) Judd is well known for her artistry with potted plants and pots and pans. She knows her onions and herbs and adds her personal flair to any recipe.

Peel or don't peel (depending on individual choice) 2 or 3 large, firm, ripe tomatoes and cut in ¼″ slices. Peel and slice 1 large onion very thin. In a shallow casserole alternate layers of sliced tomatoes and onion rings.

Dressing: In large bottle shake ½ C olive oil and ½ C vinegar, salt and pepper to taste, and if you like, add your own choice of herbs. Pour over the tomatoes and onions, cover casserole and set in refrigerator to marinate and chill well. This is excellent for a luncheon with cold meats, cottage cheese, crispy French bread, and iced tea.

"Tetta's" Salad Dressing

"TETTA" (MRS. THOMAS) RICHERT tossed this together one day!

Blend together in blender: ½ qt. mayonnaise, ½ 10½-oz. can bouillon soup, 1 2¼-oz. jar drained capers, 1 clove crushed garlic, 1 t curry powder, salt, onion, or other seasonings to taste (anchovy or soy).

Green Goddess Salad Dressing

OLLIE (MRS. R. L.) MILLER serves this dressing for her luncheon salads and hopes the women don't mind the calories!

A day or two before serving combine all ingredients in a bowl and blend well. Refrigerate in covered jar. 1 clove garlic, minced; ½ t dry mustard; 1 t Worcestershire sauce; 2 T anchovy paste; 3 T tarragon-wine vinegar; 3 T minced chives or green onions; ⅓ C minced parsley; 1 C mayonnaise; ½ C sour cream, black pepper and salt.

Eggs Florentine

On a cool day in Nuuanu Valley CATHARINE (MRS. REGINALD H.) CARTER serves a simple hot luncheon dish instead of a salad.

For each serving: place cooked, drained, chopped spinach on top of 1 piece of buttered toast. Place poached egg on top and pour over a generous portion of canned Welsh Rarebit (heated).

FISH

THE COLORFUL OLD FISH MARKETS in Chinatown are disappearing, but I can remember going there as a child with my mother. As proprietors raze the sagging, smelly sheds, they replace them with spanking new modern buildings which may look stylish and grand but, oh, how they lack the atmosphere of yore. The vendors knew they were dealing with shrewd housewives so they sold only the freshest seafood, the turnover was quick, and competition was keen. The crabs and lobsters were still crawling and the fish were still wriggling and jumping. Right from the ocean or private ponds came the colorful sea life onto the bed of handcracked ice on marble counters. Behind this glimmering array stood the fish mongers in their bloody, dirty, butcher aprons and sleazy T shirts . . . always on the alert for a sale. For the most part they were oriental men. The buyer would look to be sure the eyes of the fish were clear, the gills red, the scales moist and not easily removed, and if still in doubt he would make the fishman poke the fish to see that the flesh was firm to the touch. If, by any chance, you hesitated over John's mullet, Harry in the next stall seized the opportunity to offer in loud tones the same fish for a dime less.

There were the Hawaiian stalls, too, and each *kamaaina* seemed to have his own favorite vendor even though they sold exactly the same thing. Steaming hot *laulaus*, *pipikaula*, red salt, white salt, *limu* of all kinds (now you are lucky to find one variety), *kukui* nut balls, hot chili peppers mixed with water, vinegar, and Hawaiian salt in an old catsup bottle, gorgeous fat-belly fillets of salt salmon, generous portions of cut-up raw fish, occasionally *kalua* pig, and always *poi* that was really *poi*. The *poi* was dispensed from a huge wooden barrel and was very hard and doughlike.

There were meat stalls, too. One sold only pork and above the counters displaying pork butts, bellies, and legs hung the innards of the portly porky pig. Neighboring stalls displayed bloody hearts, livers, tripe, and sides of beef. There were special sections for the fowl—live chickens, caged and squawking, plucked chickens hanging by the head and feathered birds swinging high above the counters filled with gleaming fat chicken parts all cut ready for the pot. Turkeys gobbled during the holiday seasons. The adjoining vegetable and fruit stalls catered to the needs of all the different races with nothing but the freshest and most tempting varieties of Island produce.

This was truly living drama—in and out the characters weaved all day long, peering through the glass cases, the elders with a sharp eye to bargains and the youngsters happily tagging along with their strawberry soda water and cracked seed. Large native women and petite mama sans dispensed their frugal allowances with great care. If that fish eye staring up at Madame didn't seem too alive and clear . . . there was always Harry.

Today the local fish market men and women go early to the auction to buy their daily supply. If the wholesale price is too high for customer consumption they will pass it up and only order by special request. A dinner of fresh fish has become really quite a great treat, so careful cooking and timing is of the essence!

Hawaiian Fish Names

ahi: yellow tuna
aku: ocean bonito
amaama: mullet
a'u: marlin
kawakawa: bonito
kumu: goatfish
moi: thread fish
opelu: mackerel
o'io: bone fish
papio: young pompano
ulua: pompano

Broiled Fish

This can be very dry. Either lay strips of bacon over it or brush generously with butter. Recommended: 2 or 3 chunks (or fillets) of *mahimahi, akule, opakapaka, ono, uku,* or red snapper. Sliced lemon and chopped parsley for garnish and always tartar sauce.

Steamed Fish

Cook the fish in gently boiling water until the skin begins to break, remove to platter and pour over 2 T hot smoking peanut oil and 2 T soy. Garnish with chopped green onions and lemon. Steam the fish in a dish over boiling water with Chinese parsley, soy, ginger and garlic and black bean sauce or oyster sauce for 20 minutes depending on size. Recommended: *kumu, moi, mullet.*

Fried Fish

This is at its best when done whole in olive or peanut oil and cooked quickly to a crispy brown. You need only to sprinkle Hawaiian salt and pepper for this. If the fish is on the large side, cut in serving pieces so it won't be overcooked. Never overcook fish as it will become dry.

Dip fillets in milk or olive oil, roll in bread crumbs, salt and pepper, and fry to golden brown in hot skillet.

Soak dark meat pieces of fish in ½ C soy, slice of ginger, 2 cloves of garlic and 1 t sugar for ½ hour. Drain and fry quickly in hot oil. When time to turn the fish over, add sliced onions or chopped green onions and remaining sauce, cover and turn off heat. Or add tofu and watercress. Recommended: Any fish is good fried, be it fillets, whole, or cut crosswise.

Baked Fish

Hawaiians prefer their baked fish wrapped in *ti* leaves to retain the juices and flavor from the cooked leaves. Allow 15–20 minutes per pound in moderate oven. Place the clean fish on several large *ti* leaves which have been ribbed, sprinkle generously with Hawaiian salt outside and in, and place slice of round onion and lemon inside the belly cavity and on both sides of fish. It takes practice to wrap the fish but be sure it is securely wrapped with lots of *ti* leaves. Tie each end and the middle with string or with *ti* leaves. The water from the well-rinsed leaves will be ample to steam and bake, but you may add a little water in the roasting pan. Recommended: *kumu, mahimahi, moana, moi, papio,*

uhu, ulua, weke and the favorite of all . . . mullet.

If *ti* leaves are not available follow the above directions using tin foil, slather with mayonnaise, and wrap securely. Sheer delight!

A five pound fish stuffed with your favorite turkey dressing, seasoned, and with a few strips of bacon on top should bake in an hour. Recommended: *kumu, opakapaka, uhu, ulua.* To bake an *ono*, cut fish crosswise in chunks and fill cavity with bacon and cover with desired seasoning. Bake in 350 oven until tender. Usually takes 15–20 minutes at the most.

Lomi Salmon

This is a Hawaiian dish served at *luaus* or *poi* suppers. *Lomi* salmon and *poi* go together like bread and jelly. Select a good 1 lb. piece of fat belly salt salmon, rip off scaley skin and soak in cold water for at least 3 hours, changing the water frequently. Test to be sure it's not still too salty. Try not to cut it but with your fingers shred and pull the fish into small pieces and discard bones. Wash about 1 dozen firm, ripe tomatoes (be sure they are fresh as tomatoes can sour the whole bowl if over-ripe), drop in boiling water to peel easily and cut out core. Mash these with your fingers into small bits and mix with salmon. The salmon keeps better without onions, and you can serve a separate dish of finely chopped green onions for those who so desire. Serve very cold. You can freeze leftovers.

However, when all is said and done what true daughter or son of *Hawaii Nei* doesn't basically resort to canned salmon, sour *poi*, and raw onions? The alternatives? Canned salmon, steaming rice, and soy!

Baked Aku or Ahi Fillets

YVONNE (MRS. JOHN) ARMITAGE has found this by trial and error and many generous friends.

Have a good sized *aku* or *ahi* cleaned and filleted, leaving the skin on. Place several layers of *ti* leaves in a shallow oven pan, lay the fillets on top. Sprinkle fish with salt and pepper, dot generously with butter, lay slices of raw bacon over the fish, then thinly slice 2 lemons and place lemon slices over bacon. Cover the pan with aluminum foil and bake in a 350 oven for 1 to 1½ hours, depending on size of the fish.

Island Fried Fish

OLLIE (MRS. R. L.) MILLER's friends are delighted when she serves this dish. However, it does take last minute cooking but Ollie never seems to mind.

It's dipped in a batter for a crisp golden crust and served with hot pineapple sauce. Wash 2½–3 lbs. of fish and pat dry with paper towels and cut into pieces about 1½″ square. Marinate in ½ C soy sauce for 30 minutes, turning once or twice. Combine ½ C flour, ½ C cornstarch, ¾ C milk, 1 egg, 3 t baking powder, 1 t salt and pepper to make a thin batter about the consistency of very heavy cream.

Pour cooking oil into a heavy skillet to a depth of 1½″ or more, heat to 375 F. When ready, drain the fish of extra soy, dip quickly into the batter, drain a bit, and plunge into the hot oil. A two-tined cooking fork is the best for this. Add as many pieces as you can at one time but be sure that the temperature of the oil stays at 375 F. The fish will cook in about 2 minutes or more and the crust will be crisp, feathery and golden. Remove to a pan lined with paper toweling and keep in a warm oven until all the fish is cooked. Serve with sauce.

Sauce: Pour 2 #211 cans of pineapple chunks, syrup and all into a saucepan, stir in ¾ C sugar and heat very gently and thoroughly. Mix 1 T cornstarch with ¼ C water . . . add to heating pineapple and cook until syrup has thickened. Arrange the pineapple sauce on a warm serving platter. Place the fish pieces carefully on top. Makes 6 servings.

Fish in Sour Cream

MRS. SARAH (JAMES) WILDER was one of Hawaii's first ladies of the land . . . her charm and hospitality was famous throughout the islands and mainland. Not only was she a fabulous hostess, basically she was a top cook in the kitchen and at her kiln. Her daughter, Kinau, was indeed dear to pass along these favorite fish dishes of hers.

Place white fillets in Pyrex dish. Sprinkle with pepper, salt, and lemon juice. Cover with sour cream and sprinkle generously with grated sharp cheese. Bake 20–30 minutes in moderate oven.

Fish Chowder for 12

Slice and boil 6 lbs. fish and break in small pieces. Boil 4 or 5 large onions and 6 large potatoes together. Add the small pieces of fish to the potatoes and onions in part of the water. Boil thoroughly for several hours in double boiler. Add 1 6-oz. can of condensed milk to same quantity of water from the onions and potatoes. Add plenty of pepper.

All fish, onions, and potatoes must be boiled together until thick and more like stew than soup.

Cut 1 lb. salt pork in small cubes and fry very slowly in heavy skillet turning constantly for half hour or until crisp and there is plenty of fat. Serve piping hot cubes and fat together as gravy with chowder and pass sliced pickles and crackers.

Lomi Salmon

Sybil (Mrs. Russell C.) Throckmorton, born of the Islands and raised a true *"keiki o ka aina"* (child of the land) married an Army officer and lived away for many years. However, she never forgot her art of Hawaiian cooking and her *lomi* salmon is sheer delight.

1 lb. king salmon (salted). Soak in cold water for 3 or 4 hours, changing the water each hour. Remove the skin, hold on chopping board and shred with a tablespoon.

3 or 4 lbs. ripe tomatoes cut in 8ths. Press pieces (skin side up) on bottom of bowl to separate skin from meat. Combine with salmon, mix well, and chill. Add chopped green onions when ready to serve. Provides six servings.

Fish Dish

Boil 1½ lbs. any white fish and ¼ cup macaroni separately. Season with salt and pepper. Make a rich cream sauce and pour over boiled fish and macaroni. Serve in deep baking dish and cover with a thin layer of whipped cream (add cream just before serving so that it will not melt).

Sauce to be served separately: chop some chutney into rather small pieces. Mix with tomato catsup and flavor with Worcestershire sauce. Mix well together and serve sauce hot. Provides four servings. From the favorite recipes of Mrs. WALTER F. DILLINGHAM.

Mahimahi in Casserole

RUTHIE (MRS. L. McCULLY) JUDD, JR. is more active on the courts than in the ocean, but this fish recipe scores high.

Cream sauce for 3 lbs. fish: 6 T butter; 5 T flour; 2 C liquid ($\frac{1}{4}$ C sherry, liquid from canned mushrooms and balance in milk); 1 T grated onion; 1 t sweet basil (optional); 1 t chopped parsley; $\frac{1}{8}$ t cayenne pepper (optional); $1\frac{1}{2}$ t accent. Add flour to butter and make paste. Add liquid slowly and remaining ingredients, and transfer to double boiler and add $\frac{1}{2}$ lb. grated Parmesan cheese.

Saute fish in butter 1 min. on each side, put in casserole, top with sliced mushrooms (which you saute first in butter). Add sauce and bake in 350 oven for $\frac{1}{2}$ hour. You may add grapes.

Fish Pudding

LEINANI (MRS. E. B.) PETERSON is noted for her old-time Hawaiian recipes. A favorite luncheon dish is this fish recipe, but it must be properly steamed in a tightly covered ring mold in a pot of boiling water.

2 C scraped fish (*oio* or any soft white fish); $\frac{3}{4}$ C soft bread crumbs; $\frac{1}{2}$ C cream and enough milk to make the mixture quite moist; 4 eggs; 1 t salt; 1 t onion juice. Scrape fish from skin with silver spoon. Mix with bread crumbs, beaten egg yolks, cream, salt and pepper, and enough milk to make moist, about $\frac{3}{4}$ C. When ready to put into tin to cook, add egg whites beaten stiff and fold into pudding. Butter tin well and be sure water in which you place the mold is boiling. Boil only 25 minutes. A pudding mold with close-fitting top and tube in center should be placed directly into boiling water. (Or a plum pudding mold may be used.) "Lei" usually serves creamed shrimps in the center and with this platter a green salad, Chinese peas, and potato strings.

(Hurrah! We found that the prepared raw fish cake found in the markets could be substituted for the "scraped" fish—and it is delicious!)

Macaroni Ring with Creamed Crab

Another of LEI PETERSON's wonderful luncheon dishes.

$\frac{1}{2}$ C cooked salad elbow macaroni, 1 C scalded cream, 1 C soft bread crumbs, $\frac{1}{2}$ C melted butter, 2 minced pimentos, 1 C grated

American cheddar cheese, salt, minced parsley chopped fine, 3 eggs beaten slightly with fork. Toss all these ingredients lightly with fork and pour into greased ring mold. Set in pan of water in the oven and cook for 40 minutes at 350 until light brown. When done, unmold and fill center with creamed fresh crab. The mold is pinkish in color. Serve with green salad of lettuce, hearts of artichokes, avocado, chopped hard-cooked eggs, and toss with a tart French dressing. Pass popovers and homemade guava jelly.

Charcoal Broiled Mahimahi

DUDLEY LEWIS is a lawyer by profession but better known in the sports world for defending his reputation against the fish. Who better to tell us how to cook fish, and he graciously obliged.

Dudley prefers *mahimahi* fillets or *ono* (or the day's catch) cooked over good old fashioned *kiawe* charcoal, but you may use briquettes. The proper fire is very important, too . . . not too hot, not ashes, but medium low. For 1 lb. fillet leave the skin on and cut into liberal serving pieces. To properly fillet the fish slice in generous serving pieces at an angle against the grain. While the coals are burning down put ¼ lb. butter in a small skillet, add 2 T lemon or lime juice and dash of vermouth—set to melt on side of grill.

Place the fish fillets on "hamburger roaster"

(2 wire grills with long handles that clamp together), close and pour or brush basting sauce on top and roast with skin side down first for good crust. Cooking time depends on thickness of fish and heat of fire . . . about 5 minutes; flip and baste, flip and baste again to brown and end up skin side down. Remove from fire, open grill and use spatula to remove flesh from skin which will stick to wire, and place on warm serving platter. Pour over remaining sauce, garnish with lots of lemon, and serve with rice and soy or butter, and tartar sauce. You may make extra sauce to serve, too.

Boulabaisse

STEPHEN COOKE has come a long way in the gourmet world from those days of fabulous mud pies at Hanahauoli kindergarten! His two fish recipes are his own creations and put down in his own words.

Stephen says it's best to make this in large quantities—six or more.
1 12-oz. pkg. frozen peeled and de-veined shrimps; 1 6-oz. pkg. frozen lobster meat; 1 6-oz. pkg. frozen crab meat; 1 10-oz. can frozen fresh oysters; 1 6-oz. can of frozen clam meat; (canned sea food doesn't taste as good) and about a pound each of fresh *ulua* or *mahimahi*, swordfish and *opakapaka* . . . all de-boned, skinned and sliced into small serving pieces. Thaw frozen seafood.

In a large pot heat 3 T OLIVE OIL and saute 1 small head of celery chopped, 4 medium onions chopped, bunch of parsley chopped (regular or Chinese) until cooked. Add lobster, shrimp, crab, firm fish, and cover with water completely. Add 2 bay leaves, large pinch of oregano, the peeled rind of one orange, salt and white pepper, 3 sloshes of vermouth or white wine, and add oysters, clams and delicate fish. Bring to boil and add 1 1-oz. pkg. saffron powder, 12 "shakes" of maggi seasoning and aji. When boiling, turn to low and simmer for 10 minutes. Remove from fire. Serve in large chowder bowls with garlic bread and tossed green salad.

Fried Mahimahi

Take a good size fillet of fresh *mahimahi* . . . preferably the thick middle part. Cut across fillet into individual portions—about 1½" thick chunks. Have two bowls. One for 2 well-beaten eggs, the other for mixture of ½ flour, ½ bread crumbs, salt and white pepper and aji. Heat a big skillet, add at least ½ lb. butter and turn heat very low. Dredge fish in egg and then flour mixture, place carefully in pan, saute very slowly, turning so all four sides have been cooked. Remove fish pieces with spatula to serving dish and keep warm in oven. Add 2 "sloshes" of any dry white wine to pan to loosen drippings, leave on low and simmer. Add

slivers of macadamia nuts and saute in butter until wine has evaporated. When ready to serve, pour this sauce over fish and serve with lemon wedges dusted with paprika and garnished with parsley. (Stephen says paprika must always be stored in the refrigerator to keep its red color!) Plain boiled taro is delicious with this along with a green vegetable and a dry sauterne.

Salmon Mousse

CATHARINE (MRS. REGINALD H.) CARTER gives us a choice of either a cold or hot fish dish for luncheons.

Chill 1 13-oz. can evaporated milk then whip until volume is doubled. Add 1 T gelatin dissolved in ½ t water. Whisk well and add 1 1-lb. can of salmon which has been finely flaked. Add the salmon slowly, whisking all the time. Place in mold and set in refrigerator.

Kedgeree

Melt 4 T butter in pan and add 3 C cold cooked fish and 1½ C cooked rice. Cover and warm slowly, turn over and brown top. Serve with a thin cream sauce containing 2 diced hard-cooked eggs and generous portion of chopped parsley. Season to taste.

Tuna and Egg

The following was a favorite Japanese-style tuna dish in the WALTER FLANDERS household.

Drain and heat 1 6½-oz. can of tuna in frying pan with butter and break fish up with fork. Add about 1 t sugar and 1 T soy and when well blended add one beaten egg and scramble right into the tuna. Serve on top of steaming rice.

MEATS

HAWAIIANS LOVED TO EAT WELL, and the appreciation of good food and the use of seasonings were a part of the Hawaiian culture. They were most fastidious people in comparison to other South Sea islanders. They carefully prepared their fish and meats with various condiments (salt, *limu*, and *kukui* nut) for the best flavor.

The *imu* was the ultimate in clean cooking, as the rocks, stumps, and leaves carefully covered any soil. The *imu* could be called the original fireless cooker.

Captain Vancouver brought the first cattle to the Islands and they were *tabu* (protected by law) for many years until they became so prolific that people were allowed to kill them for food. Being wild cattle they were tough to eat, so the Hawaiians learned the art of making jerk beef and cooking it later.

For well over a century ranching has been a part of the Hawaiian way of life. The first cowboys were imported from Mexico; hence the Hawaiian word for cowboy, *paniolo*, derived from "Spaniard." The novels of Armine Von Tempsky give an authentic picture of ranch life on the outside Islands in the 20's and 30's. The Parker Ranch on the island of Hawaii has had a colorful history, and today the ranch supplies the Islands with a good portion of their prime beef.

Molokai and deer are synonymous. The small, privately-owned island of Lanai abounds in deer and Mouflon sheep. All the islands have their share of wild pigs and goats. Pigs are raised for market in rural areas and Chinese prefer Island pork in all their cooking, while the Hawaiians covet a hundred pound pig for the *imu*.

We now have federally inspected slaughter houses, which insure conformity to the same standards as mainland meat. Before commercial meat tenderizer became so popular, Island housewives wrapped their cheaper cuts of meat in papaya leaves after washing and pounding them. If left overnight the papaya juices rendered the meat choice and edible.

Hawaiians still make jerk beef, but today use large screened boxes to hang the meat or fish to dry in the full sun. This is called *pipikaula* or beef jerky.

Oven Kalua 'Pig'

You might call this "lazy man's *kalua* pig" —if nothing else it does have that unique *imu*-taste. Buy a four- or five-pound pork butt with a little extra fat. Score the fat deep in about 1″ squares, rub with white Hawaiian salt and generously sprinkle Bar-B-Q Smoke (liquid) over all sides of the meat, and especially into the fat. Clean your *ti* leaves and remove the tough center ribs to make leaves more pliable. Lay about six large leaves on a flat surface, place the well-seasoned pork butt on top and start wrapping securely like a package, adding more leaves as needed to cover completely. Tie with either *ti* leaf or string. Bake in slow 325 F oven for at least 5 hours. When fully cooked open the *ti* leaves and broil the scored fat until it is beautifully browned and crisp.

Throw in a pan of baking bananas the last

half hour, or sweet potatoes the last hour and a half, add boiled taro or taro cakes, and you have a mini *luau*. No *ti* leaves? Back to the tin foil!

The Oriental variation is simple and good, too. Mix 3 T Hawaiian salt, dash of aji, ¼ C soy, 1 t Worcestershire sauce, crushed clove of garlic and piece of crushed ginger and rub into pork, then sprinkle with liquid smoke. Wrap and cook as above.

Giant Laulaus

Individual *laulaus* can be quite a chore to make, but this discovery is simple, tastes absolutely genuine, and is easier to serve. Wash and clean 6 lbs. *luau* leaves and wash and rib a dozen or more large *ti* leaves. Have one or more 5-lb. pork butts on the fatty side well sprinkled with Hawaiian salt. Place several *ti* leaves on flat surface, stack half of luau leaves on top and sprinkle with Hawaiian salt, place pork butt on top of leaves, cover with rest of leaves to surround and then wrap with *ti* leaves to form package and tie securely. (Keep fat side up.) Place on rack in big steamer with tight cover, add water, and steam for at least five hours. Sweet potatoes and bananas may be added last hour. Be sure the water bubbles gently and constantly and add more if needed. If you think the cover is not secure, place a heavy object on the lid. Steam is important.

Hawaiian Stew with Luau

This dish seems to be a thing of the past, but there are a few old timers who will take the time and trouble to cook it as of yore because it is so delicious. In a large pot brown one lb. of Island pork cut in stewing pieces with one lb. beef stew meat (or lean brisket), sprinkle with Hawaiian salt and then add just a little water to cover and simmer until tender. In another pot cook 3 lbs. cleaned *luau* leaves about 1½ hours or until soft and remember to change the water. When both are done, drain and rinse the leaves well and combine, season with salt and pepper, and simmer for 10 minutes. Best eaten with sour *poi*, raw onions, *limu* and chili pepper!

Basic Recipe for Hawaiian Stew

Brisket makes the best stew. Remove suet not fat. Brown meat on high flame with Hawaiian salt and pepper. Add boiling water to cover and simmer 1 hour or until meat is tender. Cook the day before, refrigerate, and remove fat from top. Reheat.

Jerky or Dried Beef (Pipikaula)

Any cut of meat may be used. Sirloin tips are popular but top round is preferred. Cut meat into strips 1" thick, sprinkle with a pinch of Hawaiian salt, cover with soy and marinate for ½ hour. Hang to dry in screened dryer in hot sun for 1 day, turning once. (This freezes beautifully.) Before serving fry quickly in hot oil to brown and cut to serving pieces.

Venison

Lots of people shy away from accepting venison from happy-hunting friends because they are not sure what to do with it. It freezes very well and can be cooked in many ways. If soaked, steeped, and wined it can be delicious. Since the deer are swift of foot there really is no fat on their bones. To remedy this, soak and refrigerate the venison cuts in oil for ten days and turn daily. Day before cooking, change oil and add soy, jigger of bourbon, ginger and garlic to marinate before grilling.

Soak a venison POT ROAST overnight in ¼ C brandy, chopped white onions, bay leaf, several cloves chopped garlic, parsley, thyme, celery stalks, nutmeg, and salt and pepper. Flour and brown the roast in lots of fat in a large pot, add the strained sauce and as much red wine as you like. Simmer for several hours with carrots, whole round small onions, potatoes, and seasoning.

For BAKED venison pierce meat with kitchen fork quite deep, sprinkle with tenderizer and let stand at room temperature for 4 hours. Place the meat in the middle of enough tin foil to wrap with the following ingredients: 1 clove garlic, minced; 1 pkg. de-hydrated onion soup; 1 can cream of mushroom soup, undiluted; 1 T Worcestershire sauce; 1 can, stem and pieces, of mushrooms using juice too. Make a bundle, wrap securely and bake at 325 for 2 hours. Rice and tossed salad is all you need to go with this.

Lamb Curry

This is good only if done with lean, meaty lamb rib or neck parts and cooked the day before serving. Three or four pounds of meat isn't really too much, as it boils down. Rinse the meat, place in pot, cover with water and let this bubble and boil for about a half hour, then pour off the fatty liquid. Add fresh water to pot; several heads of garlic; small piece of ginger, slivered; 2 chopped onions; bay leaf; several T's curry powder; 1 T ginger and 1 t thyme, salt and pepper, and bring to boil and turn to simmer. Cook meat slowly until it begins to fall from the bones. Cool and refrigerate overnight. The next day hack off the lard, warm, and remove the bones, bring to boil and thicken with flour-and-water paste. Simmer to keep warm, test seasoning, and just before serving add 1 C coconut milk. (The coconut milk is what will bring your guests back for sec-

onds.) Rice, bananas, and a tossed green salad here, too.

The condiments for curry are endless, but the basics are: shredded coconut, chopped egg, chopped crisp bacon, chopped green onions, chopped peanuts, pickle relish, and the most important—mango chutney.

You can substitute stewing CHICKEN for the lamb and since this is not greasy there is no need to cool it to remove the lard. Just steam the whole bird in the water, etc. Thicken after meat is cooked and deboned, simmer and then add coconut milk.

VEAL may be used in the same way, too. Brown 2 lbs. veal cut in small pieces in ½ C oleo, add 2 sliced onions, add water to cover, your curry powder to taste, salt and pepper and cook until meat is tender. Thicken with flour-and-water paste and add 1 t vinegar. Don't forget the coconut milk before serving.

Leg of Lamb

Try rubbing a leg of lamb with curry powder, ginger, thyme, garlic, salt and pepper and roast as usual. Smells gorgeous and tastes even better.

Teriyaki Sauce

For a basic sauce for soaking or basting meat or fowl, combine ½ C soy, ½ C

Page 48: MEATS

water, 1 T brown sugar, clove crushed garlic, chopped piece ginger and jigger of bourbon.

Hawaiian Chop Suey

Ask the butcher to chop up 3 lbs. of beef or pork for chop suey. Soak this for ½ hour in enough soy sauce to cover meat and a slug of bourbon, shredded ginger finger, crushed, large clove of garlic, t of sugar, and dash of aji. Meanwhile, slice 2 large white onions, slice 1 carrot and white turnip Chinese style (on angle), string handful of beans well and slice, open 4-oz. can of mushrooms or soak a 1-oz. package of dry mushrooms, chop one bunch (4–5 stalks) of green onions in 1" lengths and wash a 12-oz. package of bean sprouts. Cut a pound block of tofu into cubes. Fry the meat in hot fat (pork longer) and then add round onions, carrot, turnip, mushrooms and string beans. Only par cook, add 2 T sugar, sauce from meat and ½ C soy, ½ C water, and bring to boil to thicken with paste of 2 T cornstarch and 1 T water. Add green onions, bean sprouts, and a little water. Taste for seasoning and correct. Add tofu, cover the pan and turn off heat. Serve with rice or over crisp noodles. (Use soy according to individual taste.)

Chicken Long Rice

This takes a lot of stock as long rice tends to soak up liquid like spaghetti. While your 4-oz. package of long rice is soaking in a large bowl of water, simmer a small stewing chicken in a qt. of water and 14-oz. can of chicken broth, 2 cloves of garlic and several slices of ginger, sliced round onion, 1-oz. package of dried mushrooms (soaked and sliced), a few dried shrimp, 1 T soy sauce, aji, and salt and pepper. When chicken is tender, remove and debone, add strained long rice to the stock . . . sure there's a lot . . . and cook about ten minutes or until tender, and add the pieces of chicken. Garnish with chopped green onions.

Hawaiian Oriental Chicken

Soak a cut-up fresh fryer for 1 hour in basic *teriyaki* sauce and keep turning to marinate well. Grill and baste over charcoal fire.

Coconut Chicken

Chicken thighs are best for this dish. Dip the parts in thawed orange juice (6 oz.) and one beaten egg and roll in mixture of 1 C bread crumbs, 1 T curry powder, and 1 C grated coconut. Place on baking pan and dribble over ¼ lb. of melted butter. Bake 45 minutes to an hour and keep in casserole. Recommended to serve to *malihinis* along with *taro* cakes, baked bananas with guava pulp and spinach and coconut milk—Hawaiian all the way.

Chicken in Papaya

Thaw 4 lbs. chicken thighs and shake thoroughly in paper bag containing flour, t salt and pepper and generous helping of curry powder (to taste). Heat electric skillet to 375, pour in ample sesame oil and brown the chicken to a golden hue. Put into large casserole with cover. When all the chicken is fried, scrape the bottom of pan and add 1 12-oz. can of papaya nectar, juice of lime or lemon, ½ of 7-oz. bottle of preserved ginger chopped in small pieces and some of the juice, salt and pepper, and brown sugar to taste. Simmer this gently for 10 minutes, stirring all the time and then add slice of ripe but firm papaya. When "gravy" smells and tastes good pour it over the chicken and cook slowly for an hour in 325 F oven. Serve with baked bananas or rice.

Hawaiian Bibi Stew

DORA (MRS. STEPHEN A.) DERBY prefaced the whole recipe by saying: "This is not for brides who have to measure teaspoons! It's a busy, busy, busy, don't let your right hand know what your left hand is doing stew . . . and great for large gatherings. And NEVER, NEVER, NEVER serve stew the day you make it."

Buy a good chuck roast and cut it in 2" cubes, bones and all, and rather bigger than smaller pieces. Shake well in a bag of seasoned flour. Brown in heavy skillet in bacon drippings until browned on all sides. Remove meat to casserole. "Deglaze" pan (scrape bottom) with a little boiling water and pour over meat. Put in 350 F oven covered. Add more bacon fat to frying pan and add a minced clove of garlic, finely chopped onion, green pepper, celery, parsley and grated raw carrot. Cook finely chopped vegetables in fat slowly until soft, stirring well. Add remaining seasoned flour from bag and enough boiling water to thicken for gravy. Season to taste with Worcestershire sauce, soy, aji, favorite herbs, salt and pepper, and fill stirring spoon with chili sauce or catsup. Pour this over the meat and add a 28-oz. can solid pac tomatoes. Keep this at 350 F until you smell it, then "throttle" to 300 F. Meanwhile back at the sink begin chopping stew vegetables: onions, green pepper, carrots, celery, bean sprouts, frozen lima beans, mushrooms, and parsley, and add to meat after it has cooked for an hour. Cook another hour or more. Remove from oven, chill, refrigerate, and next day take out all coagulated grease and remove bones. Re-heat in oven and serve with rice, tossed green salad, and French bread with herb butter. (Mix 1 stick (¼ lb.) of butter with 1 t of Spice Island Fine Herbs).

"This," adds Dora "is a vegetable stew and must taste superlative. So don't drown it if you want to add red wine." (I would say this was the mother of free-hand-optional stews.)

Coconut-Beef Stroganoff

ADEL (MRS. LYLE) BACHMAN has a new Hawaiian-Russian recipe, so to speak!

Slice 2½ lbs. either top sirloin or *teriyaki* meat in thin slices and soak in white wine overnight. Next day quickly pan broil the meat in butter and add wine, Worcestershire sauce, ½ t garlic salt, dash of spice Parisienne (use sparingly), and T boquette garni. Simmer for 1 hour or bake covered in oven at 325 F for an hour, adding water to keep from burning. Cool and add 1 12-oz. can coconut milk (thawed) and thicken with flour if need be. Keep warm and just before serving add ½ pt. of sour cream and chopped chives, and all-purpose salt seasoning. With this serve regular rice colored with tumeric powder and a separate dish of fresh or canned mushrooms warmed with white wine.

Kanaka Stew

Just looking at LAMBERT APO you know he cooks a good "*Kanaka* stew," and he told me just how he did it.

"Brisket is the best. Brown the meat with garlic and ginger and onion, if you like, add a little water and *pau*. Only easy," says Lambert. "Sometimes can add quartered cabbage the last minute or whole tomatoes, carrots and potatoes, but more *ono* plain," he added.

Chinese Style Tongue

AH TONG LEONG is the anchor man at Kahuku for Malaekahana Bay. His culinary reputation is unsurpassed.

Boil tongue until tender, cool and peel. For the sauce, brown 1 clove garlic in 2 T salad oil; add ½ C soy, 3 or 4 T sugar, pinch of Chinese 5 spices and simmer gently until tongue is well marinated and very tender. You can water down the soy if too strong. Slice and serve in gravy.

SHADA (MRS. ED) BRYAN, wife of a plantation manager, does her share of entertaining well and efficiently because she is such a good cook. She loves to create and experiment with different foods and combinations. The following three recipes are some of her experimenting.

Spare Ribs

Cut up 5 lbs. spare ribs and marinate in ½ C soy; ½ C white vinegar; 1 lg. garlic, chopped; 1 finger ginger, sliced; 2 T honey (or sugar); and the juice from a #211 can of pineapple chunks. Let stand several hours, turning occasionally. Add pineapple chunks and bake at 350 F, turn after ½ hour, turn again in ½ hour. If not done turn off oven and leave ribs in for ½ hr.
Remove ribs to bowl. Pour sauce into con-

tainer and refrigerate. Next day skim off grease, pour sauce over ribs, and heat. Add salt if necessary. Before serving add thin sliced carrot and *daikon* to cook about 10 minutes. If a thick sauce is desired, thicken with cornstarch.

Ewa Beef Riblets

Marinate 16 riblets in ½ C soy; finger of ginger, crushed; 3 cloves garlic, chopped; juice and grated rind of 1 lemon; ¼ C catsup, ½ C sauterne, and salt and pepper, for several hours or overnight. Bake 1 hour in 350 oven—turn once to brown evenly. Best if refrigerated overnight and reheated in covered casserole or pan. Yields 6 to 8 servings.

Tongue

Buy a smoked tongue. Simmer 4–5 hours with bay leaf, garlic, and 10 peppercorns. Peel and trim, then place in casserole, pour over 1 pt. sherry and add ½ C seedless raisins, 2 sticks cinnamon, 1 doz. cloves. Cover and bake at 350 for an hour and turn frequently.

Tripe Hale Ola

"DOLLY" (MRS. HERBERT G.) PANG lives in a stunning Portuguese town house (designed by the late Bert Ives) smack in the middle of Waikiki. From this elegant background comes this dressy recipe.

Wash 3 lbs. fresh honeycomb tripe in 2 or 3 changes of cold water and cut sheets of tripe into 1½" squares. Put in a lidded kettle and add 1 t salt; ½ t cracked pepper or cayenne; 1 C chili sauce; 1 T Worcestershire sauce; 2 C chicken stock, fresh or canned; 2 large Maui onions, peeled and quartered; 4 large beef tomatoes, coarsely chopped; and add more stock if necessary to cover tripe, etc. Bring to boil, reduce heat, simmer for approximately 2 hours. Meanwhile place 1" rounds of Portuguese sausage in skillet, add water until halfway mark, season lightly with salt, and cook until all water disappears. Turn off heat and let sausage stand until ready to use. Transfer tripe and all ingredients to covered earthenware casserole and add 3 or 4 halved peeled potatoes (medium size), sausages with some of the drippings from skillet, and pour over 1 C of dry red wine. Correct seasonings. Preheat oven to 250 F and cook for another 1½ hours or until potatoes are tender. Serve bubbling hot. Yields 4 to 6 servings.

Sweet Sour Spare Ribs

MRS. SARAH (JAMES) WILDER made this important footnote on the following recipe: if served with other Chinese dishes this recipe is ample for 6 servings, but if served as the main dish count on only serving three or four!

3 lbs. spareribs cut in 1½″ pieces; 2 T cornstarch; 1 T brown sugar; 1 T salt; 2 T soy sauce; 1 clove garlic, crushed; 1 slice ginger root, crushed; ½ C salad oil; 1 C vinegar; 2 T brown sugar; ½ C water. Combine spareribs, cornstarch, brown sugar, salt and soy and let stand 15 minutes or more. Sauté garlic and ginger in hot oil until brown. Add spareribs, cook until browned on all sides, then pour off excess oil. Add vinegar, remaining brown sugar, and water. Cook over high heat until steaming, then turn to low heat and simmer 30 to 40 minutes or until ribs are tender.

Portuguese Holiday Pork

MRS. LUCY MENDONCA, a Gold Star Mother and grandmother many times over, explained this recipe in great detail after she gave me a generous sample one Christmas. If you like spicy food, you'll love this, too.

It is an old Portuguese custom to serve this on Christmas morning, and the tradition is to serve with it Portuguese sweet bread, green olives, and vino—lots of it! The secret of making this dish is to use a split spoon and keep stirring and packing to marinate the meat.

Take a 4 lb. lean pork butt and cut in 1½″ pieces and put in large bowl, or better yet, a crock. In another bowl mix 6 chopped chili peppers (careful cutting so not to burn fingers or eyes); 3 large pieces of garlic, chopped small like the pepper; 2 T Hawaiian salt and 3 C white vinegar. Stir this *well* with a spoon. When thoroughly mixed pour over the meat and stir until meat is fully covered, pack down firmly and cover. This really should be started in the morning, and the more you *stir* and *stir* and turn and turn the more the meat is marinated and seasoned. So if you start in the morning, stir well and pack down again at four o'clock. After TV at 11 pm stir and pack down again. By 5 or 6 a.m. it's time for a real good toss and stir again. At 7 a.m. put 12 pieces of meat in colander to drain while deep pot with fat is heating. When good and hot drop in the meat, cover half way for 15 minutes, fry and stir 15 minutes until juice is all out and meat browns. Remove to another pot or casserole. Repeat another drained 12 pieces until all the meat is in casserole or pot and put in oven to cook thoroughly and keep warm.

With a twinkle in her eye she added: "This makes 'num-num' *pupu* if you sliver the meat instead of cubing it and fry it until crispy and well done—and don't forget the wine or beer, if you please!

Hawaiian Stew

ERNEST K. KAI, an outstanding son of Hawaii *Nei*, is a lawyer by choice and gourmet by birth. His Chinese oven has been featured in national magazines along with many of his recipes. However, locally he is famous for his Hawaiian stew, and like all good cooks he had a time "writing" it down.

2 lbs. chuck steak (cut in chunks); 1 medium onion; 2 large or 3 medium ripe tomatoes; 2 C cold water; 2 carrots. Dry the meat on paper towels. Sprinkle with about one level T Hawaiian rock salt and pepper to taste. Heat oil (bland flavored) in pan which will be used for the cooking, preferably a Dutch oven. (If not use a flat bottom frying pan.) Fry the meat and the onions together *only* until the redness turns greyish—DO NOT BROWN—then add the 2 C water. (If done in frying pan scrape well to remove meat and gravy and put in stew pot.) Cover and simmer for about an hour. Add quartered tomatoes. Check water, if not enough add more. Simmer for another hour. Add the carrots cut in chunks, about 20 minutes before the end of cooking time.

Because the "gravy" is unthickened and therefore thin, this stew is best eaten in a large soup bowl with knife, fork and soup spoon. Accompanying foods should be on their own plates. *Especially good accompanied by poi.*

Wine Hash

"Lei" (Mrs. E. B.) Peterson recommends this hash for a hearty dinner—en famille or company.

Brown 1 T flour in 2 T butter, add 1 large chopped onion, and slowly fry. Add 1 garlic clove, minced; 1 green pepper, chopped; and 1 large tomato, chopped. Thin with 1 C white wine and a little broth. Last of all add 2 C cooked meat, either chopped or cut up, and 1 t minced parsley. Add pepper generously and salt sparingly. Simmer for half an hour or until well blended. The hash can be served in the middle of a ring mold of green rice or mashed potatoes generously sprinkled with chopped parsley.

Butterfly Leg of Lamb

Jack (Mr. John C.) Walker is a genial host, and stars at the barbecue, especially.

Have the butcher bone a leg of lamb, boil the bones with onion and celery, and save. Marinate the lamb in dry wine—Burgundy or claret—rosemary powder, and grated onion for at least a half a day.

If cooked on spit, roll the lamb with chopped mushrooms, tie, and baste with marinade. Add juice to stock and thicken for gravy. When cooking over charcoal, baste well with marinade and broil skin side down first and baste constantly. Cook as you would a steak —rare, medium, or well done. Thicken the lamb stock for gravy and season to taste.

Jack Walker's Steak Sauce

½ lb. soft butter, 1½ T dry mustard, 2 T

Worcestershire sauce, 1 T A-1 sauce . . . mix all well and spread on steaks to broil.

Beef & Tomatoes

L. McCully Judd, Jr. was kind enough to take four hours to prepare this recipe for publication, because he says, "I am a by-gosh and by-golly cook." Normally, he tosses this off at the drop of a hat.

3 lbs. meat (all beef, or 2 lbs. beef and 1 lb. belly pork, Island); 6 medium onions, wedge-cut in eights; 2 bunches (4–5 stalks each) green onions, cut ½"; 4–5 stalks celery, outside pieces, slit and cut into ½" length; 7 large tomatoes, cut in small wedges and halved; 2 bell peppers, sliced; 2 C fresh mushrooms, sliced; 4–5 cloves garlic put through press.

In hot skillet (350) put 5 T oil, add garlic, stir, and add 1 lb. belly pork sliced thin. Cook fast, stirring all the time, and smell to be sure that garlic essence is there. (You can overcook pork and make it tough.) 5 minutes should do it. Add the 2 lbs. of sliced beef and keep temp. at 375 to sear fast—don't overcook. Sprinkle ½ C soy over meat, dash of aji, and remove after 10 minutes to bowl. Remove the meat with spatula so the gravy remains in the pan. To hot pan add onions, celery, green pepper, juice of 5 oz. can sliced mushrooms, 2 C fresh mushrooms and cover to simmer for 15 minutes. Thicken

with 4 T cornstarch mixed with water for paste. Careful in pouring as it thickens quickly. Return meat to pan, rinse bowl with water and add for gravy, plus can of mushrooms. Now taste for seasoning and salt to taste. Add tomatoes and green onions. Salt to taste, stir, turn over quickly, and serve hot over rice. McCully serves this with a tossed salad.

Salad

Wash 3 heads of fresh lettuce and crispen in refrigerator. Dressing: 1 lg. clove garlic, using press; 4 T olive oil; 2 T lemon; 2 T wine vinegar; 1 t mint sauce, and 1 t salt—cuts acidity. When ready to serve, add 3 T Parmesan cheese; 4 slices bacon well fried and chopped; croutons made from 2 slices of bread spread with garlic butter and toasted in oven; add to broken lettuce and toss with dressing. Pass salt and ground pepper.

* * * * *

McCully suggests trying this: rub a leg of lamb with soy before roasting!

Mint Sherbet

(To serve with roast lamb)
Pound leaves of one bunch (½ cup) of mint. Add juice of 2 lemons. Let it stand for 15 minutes. Boil 2 C sugar and 1 pint water till it threads. Stir all together. Let cool and freeze. From the favorite recipes of Mrs. Walter F. Dillingham.

Soy Sauce for Steaks

1 qt. bottle soy; 1 small ginger root, grated fine; 1 large or 2 small cloves garlic, grated; 1 T brown sugar; 1 T dry mustard; 2½ oz. *oke* or bourbon. Mix all ingredients. Put in large pan and soak steak in mixture ½ hour on each side before broiling. Mixture can be bottled, kept in ice box, and used several times. From the fevorite recipes of Mrs. WALTER F. DILLINGHAM.

Pork Chops

KINAU WILDER has a marvelous faculty for crashing through with a brilliant dramatic punch line—something she's learned behind the footlights all these years, no doubt. The instructions for the pork gravy is a coup, and the curry recipe is typical of her surprise lines!

Use only double center-cut pork chops 1½″ thick. Marinate them all day (on the counter) in sauce of 1 C soy, 1 C vinegar, 1 C brown sugar, garlic and grated ginger root, or if none available use candied or crystalized ginger, and heaping T dry mustard. Be around to keep turning and marinate well. Broil in oven on lower rack for long time to be sure pork is cooked, and baste occasionally. Serve with baked potatoes and instead of using butter dribble the basting sauce over the halves!

Fool-Proof Curry

In a pot put ¼ lb. butter and fry 2 large onions, chopped; 2 fingers of ginger and garlic cloves, chopped. Add one 2-oz. bottle of curry—"the more the merrier"—and cook it all up. Take this mixture, put in blender and add one can of ready-to-use white sauce (about 1¼ cups) and a 12-oz. can of frozen (thawed) coconut milk! When nicely blended to right consistency put in top of double boiler to keep hot.

Cook your chicken by steaming, de-bone, and add large hunks of the chicken to sauce.

SIMPLE! With rice, condiments and green salad.

Hawaiian Style Curry

MRS. LYLE BACHMAN not only gave me a superbly different curry recipe but generously threw in the rest of the dinner which she generally serves to her *malihini* friends.

1 qt. frozen coconut milk; ½ C passion fruit juice; ½ C guava juice; ½ C fresh chicken stock or 2 cubes chicken bouillon melted in ½ C water; 1 t soy; dash aji; 1 t tumeric for coloring. Simmer this altogether and thicken with 2 T of the packaged Chinese starch mixed with a little liquid and 2–4 T curry—depending on how hot you like it.
Clean 3½ lbs. shrimps and sprinkle with

seafood seasoning. Add them to the sauce and if too thick don't use water but cow's milk to dilute to right consistency. Slowly simmer for 20 minutes stirring frequently, add 1 T Spice Parisienne and stir to distribute evenly. Set aside. Put in casserole for serving and bake in oven for ½ hour. She added that the passion and guava juice is optional.

Instead of serving regular rice she mixes a box of long grain wild rice mix and 2 6-oz. packages of chicken-flavored rice and cooks all together. As for the condiments she stresses the tiny Japanese sweetsour pickled scallions sliced very thin, chopped macadamia nuts, pickled pineapple, chutney, and shredded coconut besides the chopped eggs, bacon, etc. With this she serves a green salad—anything green including avocados —with a sweet sour dressing. Butter rye bread slices with garlic butter, wrap in tin foil and serve hot. For dessert she completes the color picture with either sliced mangoes or papaya with watermelon.

Hawaiian Curry

Grate 1 coconut, squeeze out the cream. Put 1 T butter into a saucepan, melt. Then add 1 onion, 1 clove of garlic, 1 small piece of ginger root, all of which have been chopped fine. Simmer until soft. Then add 1 T of dry curry powder and 4 T flour. Stir together into a paste. Add slowly 1 qt. of milk, into which you have put the coconut cream. Stir slowly until all the milk is used, then put into double boiler with pieces of a cooked four-pound chicken. Salt to taste. Provides 6 servings.

These condiments were listed for a lobster curry: chopped green peppers, grated coconut, chopped pickled onions, chopped hard-cooked eggs, Bombay duck (crisped in oven), crisp bacon chopped fine, chopped preserved ginger, mango chutney, and chopped roasted nuts. From the favorite recipes of Mrs. Walter F. Dillingham.

Curry Sauce

Cleo (Mrs. Robert) Evans is not only noted for her chic and good taste in clothes, but for her superlative taste in gourmet cooking. The following two recipes are unusual, easy and good.

1 chopped onion, 1 stalk celery, 2 cloves garlic, ½ green apple, chopped (or tamarind, if available), 4 T flour, 2 C milk (use coconut milk if making shrimp curry and chicken broth if making chicken curry), salt, marjoram, thyme, savory, bit of crushed fresh ginger, curry powder, aji.

Sauté onion, apple and celery in 2 T oil and 2 T butter. Add ginger and garlic. Add good pinches of the herbs, and curry powder to taste (2 or more ts). To thicken add flour; then slowly add milk or other liquid.

Broiled, Baked, or Barbecued Chicken

1 C salad oil, ⅓ C lemon juice, 3 T soy, 2 cloves garlic, crushed; 1 t oregano; ¼ t aji; ½ t salt; ¼ t pepper (for marinade). Four- to six-pounds chicken (thighs, breasts, or split broilers). Crush garlic in roasting pan, add all other ingredients and mix well. Put chicken in marinade for at least four hours. For *outdoor grilling* put chicken on grate and baste sparingly. For *baking*, pour off most of marinade and bake at 400 about 30 minutes. For *indoor broiling*, remove from marinade and place on broiling rack.

Chicken in Spinach and Coconut

BETH (MRS. FRANK W.) BROADBENT was brought up on a ranch on Hawaii, and the Chinese cook, Asam, would throw her bodily out of the kitchen if she dared step foot in his domain. So this dish is truly her own spe- cialty, and I'm sure will soon have *luau* leaves a drug on the market.

Thaw completely: 2 1-lb. packages frozen chicken thighs and drumsticks, 2 10-oz. pack- ages frozen chopped spinach, 1 12-oz. can coconut milk. Add to coconut milk: 1 can cream of chicken soup, 1 t onion chips, 1 t sugar. In a casserole place first the spinach, then the chicken and pour on the liquid. Bake in open dish at 375 for 1½ hours. Later add a little cornstarch and salt.

Chicken Luau

SYBIL (MRS. RUSSELL C.) THROCKMORTON is another Big Island ranch girl! You can be sure her recipes are tried and true.

Simmer slowly a 1-lb. box thawed chicken breasts and 1 1-lb. box chicken thighs 'til done, in water with: 2 stalks celery, garlic to taste, salt to taste, 2 t chicken stock sea- soning or 1 chicken bouillon cube. When done strain liquid and save.

Wash 2 lbs. or more *luau* leaves, cut off an inch of each leaf tip, peel large stems, cover with water in large pot and boil for an hour. Drain, cover with fresh water, and boil until easily cut with spoon. Drain.

Combine chicken and *luau*, and add 1 pint or more frozen coconut milk (thawed). Add ½ t (or more) sugar. Heat thoroughly in double boiler. Provides 6 servings.

"Lei Moni" Chicken

I apologized to DIANE (MRS. ARTHUR C.) SLOGGETT for not pressing her for a Kama- aina recipe, and she was quick to respond with. . . . "But Artie has a divine recipe." And here it is!

3 1-lb. boxes chicken thighs, thawed; ⅓ C flour; 2 t oregano; 1 small garlic clove, mashed; 2 T salad oil; ½ C catsup; ½ C lemon juice; 2 T chopped onion; ½ t black pepper; ½ t thyme. Dredge chicken pieces

in flour and oregano. Melt shortening in skillet and brown chicken pieces on all sides. Transfer to casserole. Combine remaining ingredients and pour over chicken. Cover and bake at 350 for an hour. (Find the title in the ingredients?!)

Poulet Truffe a l'Armagnac

STEPHEN COOKE has two special dishes he makes for his family and friends. His chicken recipe may not be for the "budget-wise housewife," but his hamburgers are sure to intrigue!

Buy 2 plump roasters, 1 2¾-oz. can pâté de foie gras, and 1 can of (4) truffles (2 per bird), and you might say this was the expensive part!

Into a large bowl put: "2 fistfuls" inside of sour dough bread (no crust) which has been soaked in a little milk and squeezed; 1 medium onion finely chopped; ½ C smoked ham finely chopped; the chopped liver, gizzards (pared) and hearts from birds; ¼ nutmeg grated; can of pâté; finely chopped truffles, plus the water; salt and white pepper to taste; several dashes of Maggi seasoning; 2 eggs and 2 hearty "sloshes" of brandy. Then mix, mix, and mix with fingers.

Preheat oven to 175 F. Stuff birds, skewer or sew cavity, smear with soft butter, and sprinkle with salt and white pepper and place on X-shaped rack over pan to bake in oven

for 5–6 hours. It will be done when beautifully browned after this long, low, and slow cooking! Baste every hour or so. Hour before finished, dust bird completely with mushroom powder—completely. Then one more baste before serving.

Gravy: Put necks and gizzard parings, 2 14-oz. cans chicken broth, 1 small chopped onion, sprig celery chopped fine, "slosh" of vermouth into pot, bring to boil and simmer until cooked. After you remove chicken to serving dish (leave in oven which has been turned off to keep warm), put pan on top of stove and add broth. Simmer to loosen drippings and stir. Thicken with 2 T arrowroot and water, strain if you like, and serve separately. This is best served with long grain white rice.

Gourmet Hamburger

Stephen emphatically says: "Use lean ground round with no fat and allow ½ lb. meat per person, at least." This recipe is for 1 lb. meat and can be doubled, tripled, or whatever!

Soak 3 T minced onion for ten minutes in just enough warm water to cover. Take out inside of day-old sour dough French bread, about the size of 2 fists (no crust), and soak in bowl of lukewarm water.

Into a large bowl put: finely chopped leaf end of a stalk of celery; handful of either

Chinese or regular parsley finely chopped; 2 very large mushrooms (not canned) finely chopped; the soaked onion; the bread which has been gently squeezed of liquid; and the meat. Add salt and white pepper, good dash of Worcestershire sauce, 6 shakes of Maggi seasoning (this is Alsace-Lorraine's answer to ajinomoto but they don't know it), ½ nutmeg, grated; 1 T powdered mushroom, and 2 raw eggs. Now mix, mix, mix very thoroughly, add a "slosh" of fine cognac and mix further. Let this stand 20 minutes to marinate. Mix again and form into thin patties.

Heat big skillet, add ½ lb. butter and keep fire low. Place patties in pan and press down so they are flat and cook 5 minutes on each side. Before removing patties, flambé with brandy, swish around in pan away from fire until it is all burned up. Put in warm oven.

Loosen drippings in pan with 1 14-oz. can beef broth, scrape, and simmer. Thicken with 2 T arrowroot powder mixed with water in a glass (cover glass with hand and shake). This sets very fast so stir quickly. Pour over meat and serve. Rice is a must accompaniment. These patties are surprisingly crunchy.

Naka's Long Rice

MURIEL (MRS. WALTER E.) FLANDERS had the most lovable and devoted *mama-san* take care of the girls when they were young.

Naka-san was an "institution" and would cook occasionally. Muriel says her long rice is not white and watery like *luau* style, but golden and comparatively dry like the kind you buy in a delicatessen. The spare ribs are delicious, too, and could be served as *pupus*.

Soak 1 1-oz. pkg. of Japanese dried mushrooms in water for 15 minutes. Soak 1 2-oz. pkg. dry shrimps for 5 or 10 minutes. Drop a couple of 2-oz. bundles of long rice in boiling water for a minute or two, drain and cut with scissors.

Fry 1 lb. *teriyaki* pork, or cut-up pork, and finely sliced onions in pan with enough oil to brown well. Add the long rice, mushrooms, shrimps, and sliced green onions. Pour "barbecue soy sauce" or soy with sugar and ginger powder (to taste) over all, mix, and cover. Let it steam until pork is fully cooked and long rice is tender. If needed, add diluted soy or plain water.

Cantonese Spare Ribs

Crush 1″ green ginger root and ½ clove garlic in pan. Blend in ½ C soy, ¾ C sugar, ½ C catsup, 2 oz. sherry, and 1 t salt. Mix sauce well and rub it into a section of young pork loin back ribs and marinate for 3–4 hours or longer. Place ribs on rack in a 325 oven and cook ¾ hour. Place a shallow pan of water under ribs to catch falling juices. Use balance of sauce for basting. Remove from oven, cut up each rib and serve hot.

Corn Beef

PEGGY MAE (MRS. ROBERT) HUNTER, born of the Islands, has spent most of her life on ranches—Maui, California, and Hawaii. As a consequence she is an expert on game and meat and has corned her own beef.

Buy the better cuts of meat (round, rump, and sirloin tip. She herself likes brisket for the bone and gristle)—5 or 6 lbs.

In a large crock put 8 C water, 1 C Hawaiian salt, 3 T sugar, 3 or 4 bay leaves, 1 1⅛-oz. bottle pickling spices, 4 large whole cloves of garlic and ¼ t saltpeter. Add the meat to the brine and cover with suitable lid and place weight on top so it is pressed down securely. "PM" said she would lift the lid and turn the meat to marinate if she thought of it or went by the crock. Let it stand for 36 hours in a COOL PLACE. Then cook as any other corned beef by boiling until tender, about 3–4 hours, changing the water occasionally.

VEGETABLES

THE RAISING AND PREPARATION of food was man's work in the early days of Hawaii! (We've come a long way.) *Taro*, sweet potatoes, breadfruit, yams, and bananas were cooked in the *imu* or underground oven which meant firewood, heavy stones, and cutting down banana stumps and *ti* leaves. The women took care of the children, wove *lauhala*, and pounded out *tapas* for wearing apparel. From what one sees in old pictures, these women had more fun and games with the kiddies and spent more time gossiping over the mats than pounding fibers!

One of the earliest cultivated crops in Hawaii was *taro*, a tuberous root grown in muddy patches and related to the elephant ear. Hawaiian *taro* can still be bought in the markets, even though most of it is used commercially to make *poi* and *taro* chips. Some people simply cannot peel the *taro* or the leaves, as the combination of vegetable and water can cause severe itching. One recommended way of cooking the root is to scrub it well, boil for several hours, changing the water two or three times, until tender and done, then peel. Another method is to peel the *taro* first, cut in half and boil like potatoes until cooked. Cooking with the skins on naturally retains the nourishment. Fork test *taro* like potatoes.

When the *taro* is cooked, you can slice in ½″ thick rounds and fry to brown in hot butter (with a little oil to keep from burning)—the crisper the better.

Taro Cakes

Boil the *taro* until very tender and mash while hot with potato masher, mix in a little water, add a scant teaspoon of baking powder, 1 t sugar and lots of butter. When well mashed and smooth, form the *taro* into small cakes with wet hands, place on buttered pan, poke a dent in each cake and press in butter. Bake at 350 F for 20 minutes or until brown. Best if you place pot over low heat when mashing and adding ingredients as it MUST be mashed HOT!

Taro Puffs

Mash 2 C of HOT *taro*, add 2 t baking powder, 1 t salt, ½ C flour and work with hands until thoroughly mixed. Form into small balls and place in small buttered muffin tin. Make a dent and press in the butter, bake in 475 F oven for 10–15 minutes until they puff and brown.

Taro Biscuits

Combine 1 C HOT mashed *taro*, ¼ C fat, blend and add 1½ C flour, 3 t baking powder,

2 t sugar and ½ t salt sifted together. Mix together with 1 beaten egg and ¼ C milk. Knead like biscuit dough on floured board and form to ½″ thickness, cut with cutter and bake 15 minutes in 425 oven.

Cubed *taro* is a change from potatoes in stew and tends to thicken the gravy. For another potato substitute at dinner, bake ½″ thick slices of cooked *taro* on baking sheet with salt and pepper and brush with butter. Brown and crispen in 375 F oven for 20 minutes. Turn once and serve hot with lots of butter.

Poi

Made from the *taro* root, *poi* is the staff of life to the Hawaiians. Years ago men pounded and kneaded the cooked *taro* by hand with a special rock called (oddly enough) a *poi* pounder. Today it is made and sold commercially. Before the war thick *poi* came bagged in white cotton material and needed a lot of water and mixing before eating. The old *poi* bag had many uses and was excellent for straining the *luau* leaves or guava pulp for jelly. Because the *poi* was full of *taro* fiber, it had to be strained after mixing, and every home had a *"poi* strainer" hanging on the clothes line. It was a square yard of crinoline and had to be properly rinsed and cleaned after each use. Today, if you can find it, *poi* comes in cellophane bags and is watered down to a point where not much water or mixing is needed and there is no reason to strain it. Some liken it to soup!

Poi is highly recommended by doctors as it is one of the most nearly perfect foods for any age. Mothers in Hawaii start their babies on *poi* and milk at six weeks, and older children love it like cereal with sugar and milk.

To remove the *poi* from the cellophane bag, open the sack and add water to loosen it from the sides, squeeze off excess water, and invert the sack of *poi* into a large wet bowl (*poi* will stick if put in dry container), add water gradually and mix by hand. Do it right under the faucet so you can control the flow easily. Slap, knead, scrape, whatever comes naturally, but keep scraping from the bottom and sides of the bowl in a beating action until it is of one or two finger consistency. As children we were always told to *"kahi the poi,"* which simply means to wipe the sides of the bowl clean and sprinkle water on the top when you are *pau*.

Today the *poi* seems to take forever to sour. If you like it sweet and fresh keep it in the refrigerator, but if you prefer it tart and tangy and practically bubbling from age, leave it covered to sour on the counter.

Poi, instead of flour and water, is good to thicken stews.

Apply *poi* to bee bites and it takes the sting and throb away.

Luau Leaves

Besides the *taro* root, the large green leaves that sprout above the mud are also edible. These, too, can cause itching and should be stripped when dry and then rinsed to clean. It is quite a process to clean the leaves properly. You must peel off the thickest part of the mid-rib (stem and veins which spread into the large leaf) and snip off the tips of each leaf end. There is a variety called Tahitian *taro* which grows in dry land. It is raised strictly for the leaves and the root is not edible. Every home garden should have a patch as it grows quickly and can be washed and cooked without thought of the *"maneo."* Hawaiian *luau* leaves can be bought in the markets, but unfortunately there is no Tahitian *luau* sold commercially.

To cook Hawaiian *luau* leaves, stuff them into a big pot with about a quart of water. They soon wilt down to a mere nothing. Simmer for an hour or more, changing the water twice with hot water until tender and thoroughly cooked. The leaves turn a sad greenish yellow and should be drained completely of all water before serving alone or in other Hawaiian dishes. *Luau* is very similar to spinach and, if served as a vegetable, just chop and add butter and seasoning. To save time and trouble many people use frozen spinach when a Hawaiian recipe calls for *luau* leaves.

Tahitian *luau* takes less time to prepare and cook. It seems to retain its bright green color and needs only about 15 minutes to cook. Drain it well, chop or puree, and serve plain with seasoning or coconut milk.

Coconut Spinach

Cook three 10-oz. packages frozen chopped spinach and drain completely of water—cheesecloth is excellent for this. Add 1 C coconut milk and salt and pepper to taste and warm to serve.

Rice

In most *kamaaina* homes the kitchen was the domain of the Chinese cook. These men were responsible for making rice the popular starch of our daily diet. To this day it is served as a matter of course and eaten with butter or soy or both. It is infinitely more popular than potatoes or bread. The secret to good, dry rice is to bring it to a boil, turn the fire down low and let the pot steam with the lid on until cooked and kernels are separated. One faithful cook almost quit in a towering rage because one of the young boys had gone through the kitchen, lifted the steaming rice pot cover, and ruined the whole lot!

Fried Rice

A perfect solution for leftover rice. Fry up several pieces of sliced bacon or leftover ham or pork; add diced onion, slivered celery, and when cooked add the rice. Stir around and break down so chunks are broken up and well mixed with other ingredients. Pour soy over, the amount depending on your taste, break in 2 eggs and keep stirring to cook the eggs, cover and steam over low fire for 20 minutes. Add chopped green onions and sliced sweet pork before serving.

Fried Bananas

Peel, scrape off strings, slit lengthwise, and fry over medium heat in lots of butter or oleo until golden brown. Try it with bacon and eggs for breakfast—the bacon flavor is great. For a new taste treat, try pouring a 6-oz. can of thawed guava concentrate over a dozen fried bananas and put in casserole to warm.

Baked Bananas

These are best when over-ripe and black. Wash and place unpeeled in baking pan with a little water for 20–30 minutes at 350 F. The skins will pop . . . then just drop in lots of butter to serve.

Glazed Bananas

These seem to complement curry. Peel 8 cooking bananas and cut in half lengthwise. Place in oiled pan: add 3 T oleo, ½ C guava jelly, little lemon juice, and water. Bake in 350 F oven for 20–30 minutes or until soft. You can gussy this up with shredded coconut before serving. Instead of lemon, try Chinese orange juice for a change.

Baked Papaya

Try this with leg of lamb, especially. Select almost ripe, firm papayas, cut in half, remove seeds and fill with pat of butter, sprinkling of cinnamon and nutmeg, 1 t brown sugar and squeeze of lime, lemon or Chinese orange juice. Bake at 250 F for ½ hour.

Breadfruit

This can be found in the market occasionally. For BAKED BREADFRUIT a thoroughly ripe one should be used. To keep your oven and pan clean, place fruit on a liberal piece of tin foil over the baking pan. Cook at 350 F for an hour minimum or until the stem pulls out very readily. If not thoroughly cooked, breadfruit can be stringy. Remove from oven and place tin foil and breadfruit on layers of newspaper. Since the rind is milky and sticky, it is a rather messy job removing the hot, soft pulp. Remove stem, scoop and scrape out meat, place in buttered casserole with ample butter, and serve hot.

Breadfruit can also be steamed or peeled and boiled until well done. Peel ripe breadfruit, core, and cut into cubes. Simmer in minimum of water in covered pot, adding more if needed. When tender, drain off liquid and add coconut cream and serve hot.

After boiling whole breadfruit slice in ½″ pieces and fry in hot oleo or butter.

My grandmother added cooked breadfruit to her stews instead of potatoes. She also made *poi* from the breadfruit—*poi ulu*—which was a gorgeous yellow color, divine looking, thicker than *taro poi*, but oh, such a taste! Unique and definitely an acquired taste! I wonder how the tourist would react to this *poi* which is rarely found today.

There are literally dozens of varieties of breadfruit in the Islands, and their eating qualities vary greatly.

Watercress

With sweeping progress, new highways, new homes, and high land taxation, the colorful old swampy watercress patches in rural areas are rapidly being filled in, but watercress can still be bought in the markets. The Japanese serve watercress as a cooked vegetable with soy. Wash the whole bunch well and either blanch quickly or pour boiling water over all, drain and chop in 3″ lengths and sprinkle with aji. Excellent with warm rice and fish.

Chinese Peas

Not only very delectable but very expensive —ranging in price from 97 cents per pound to $2.50, and when properly strung you wonder what you bought! These peas must be properly and utterly strung otherwise they are just so much pulp. Cook with minimum of water and bring to a boil, remove from fire for a few minutes, drain and add butter and seasoning. It is best to undercook them and enjoy their flavor and crunchiness. These are the same peas whose seeds are sold under the name of edible-podded peas. All vegetables should be picked young, but especially Chinese peas.

Soy Beans

These beans are sold in the market by the bunch—stems, leaves, and the fuzzy pods. Strip beans from branches, wash well, and cook quickly in salted water for about ten minutes. Rinse, drain, and leave in icebox for nibbling—protein galore.

Sarah Wilder's Baked Bananas

Peel 4 bananas, cut in halves, place in baking dish, sprinkle with juice of ½ orange, 2 T sugar and ½ t cinnamon. Scatter bits of butter over all and bake in moderate oven 1 hour. If they bake dry add more orange juice.

Taro Cakes

SHADA (MRS. ED) BRYAN adds a new twist to her *taro* cakes when she adds Portuguese sausage and passes them as *pupus*.

Boil 2 good-sized or three small *taro* roots until tender. Peel, and while hot put through ricer adding 2 T butter so it will melt. Mix *taro* and butter with fork and over this shake with sieve 1 t sugar, ½ t salt, 2 t baking powder. This sifting *does* make a difference. At this point shred Portuguese sausage with a fork and add to mixture. Make small flat cakes size of teaspoon and bake in 400 F oven for 25 minutes. If making plain *taro* cakes, form into flat cake, make hole and dab in the butter. Cook at 350 oven for 45 minutes. These are crispy. Shada says the less handling the better.

Parsley Tempura

SHADA (MRS. ED) BRYAN grows her own parsley and makes a melting-in-the-mouth *tempura* with these large green sprigs.
Use a large bowl and mix ½ C flour, ½ C cornstarch, ½ t baking powder, ½ t salt, 1 C water, and beat until smooth. Dip fresh, large sprigs of parsley into batter, shake off excess and fry quickly in deep fat.

Taro Cakes

JACK (MR. JOHN C.) WALKER takes the cold approach to *taro* and stresses the importance of taking cakes from icebox directly to oven.

Select white *taro* and cook until tender. Cool and put through food chopper. Mix with little salt to taste and lots of butter. Form into balls with "well buttered hands" and place well spaced (they spread) on buttered pan. Put in icebox. When ready to serve, preheat oven to 400 F and take pan from refrigerator and place immediately in hot oven and bake for 20 minutes to half an hour until they puff and brown. These may be frozen.

Onion Pie

Leila (Mrs. James F.) Morgan, Jr. has lived on several plantations and is adept at the art of preparing last minute meals or detailed planned menus. This onion recipe is one of her popular vegetable dishes.

Make crust with 1¼ C soda cracker crumbs and ⅓ C melted butter or make regular pie crust—this is better, naturally. Slice 2 C onions thin. Fry in 2 T butter or margarine. Cook soft but not brown. Place onions in crust. Make a custard with 1 C scalded milk into which you've slowly stirred 2 slightly beaten eggs, 1 t salt, ¼ t pepper. Add 1½ C grated cheddar cheese. Pour into crust over onions. Bake in 300 F oven for 40–45 minutes or until done by cake tester.

Kanamatsu's Scrambled Egg And Tomato

Muriel (Mrs. Walter E.) Flanders remembers her grandmother MacFarlane's old cook, Kanamatsu, who graduated from the Boston Cooking School around the turn of the century. He always served this on Sunday morning after church at the Waikiki house.

• Slice 2 tomatoes (skin left on) in thin slices and cook in a little butter in frying pan. Mash with fork until well done, rather brown, and quite dry. Then pour in 6 beaten eggs and scramble. Important: don't add water or milk to the beaten eggs as it will get watery. *Just* eggs.

Red Cabbage

Mrs. Sherwood Lowrey had a special way of cooking red cabbage that her children still serve today.

2 small red cabbages, finely shredded; 4 tart green apples, sliced; 3 T butter; 4 T wine vinegar; ½ C brown sugar; 6 whole cloves; 6 peppercorns; 1 onion, chopped; 1 clove garlic optional. Saute chopped onion and sliced apples in butter and when done add all ingredients except the cabbage. Simmer 15 minutes and add cabbage to cook about 30 minutes to an hour, depending on your taste. Mrs. Lowrey preferred to simmer it at least an hour, but some may prefer it crunchier.

FRUITS & PRESERVES

BY AND LARGE, such mainland fruits as apples, peaches and pears do not thrive in Hawaii, even at higher elevations, but in their place we have a magnificent variety of tropical and semi-tropical fruits.

The lacy-leafed TAMARIND tree looms up occasionally, but few people recognize or appreciate it. (My mouth waters just thinking about that acidy fruit.) The brown outside shell is brittle and inside the meat clings to shiny seeds. A basic syrup is made from this fruit.

Ages ago a MULBERRY tree seemed to grow in every garden, but now only a few. It was mostly a losing battle with the birds for the black, sweet fruit, delicious with sugar and cream or made into pie.

Another common sight was the purple ISA-BELLA GRAPE tumbling over wooden trellises. Introduced over 150 years ago it flourished for many years, but today you rarely see well-tended grape vines.

The MOUNTAIN APPLE, brought by the early Hawaiians, still thrives in lush valleys. The feathery blossoms are a gorgeous laven-der red and the fruit crimson with thin skin and white flesh. Delightful to eat right from the tree, especially on long hikes, as it is crisp and juicy but with little nutrition. In summer the rural roads are dotted with enterprising road-sellers. Due to lack of pectin or flavor these do not make jelly but can be pickled.

The OHELO BERRY is one of the oldest fruits of Hawaii and is identified mostly with volcanoes and Madame Pele on the island of Hawaii. Ohelo may be eaten raw or cooked for sauce or pie.

FIG trees were brought to the Islands in the early nineteenth century, and by the looks of some of the old gnarled trees they may be the originals. Birds have found them a tasty fruit, too, thereby discouraging their cultivation. Figs are easily bruised when picked dead ripe, but delicious peeled and served with sugar and thick fresh cream.

We have a JAVA PLUM tree in our yard, and but for hiding an ugly telephone pole with its green, shiny foliage it would have gotten the ax years ago! The olive-shaped purple fruit has no pectin, is very bitter, creates a purple-stained mess for weeks, and so is generally unpopular.

BREADFRUIT was brought to Hawaii from Tahiti where it was the staff of life for the natives. The tree is tall and stunning with its heavy foliage of big spike-shaped leaves. Samoans in Hawaii cruise around in search of the trees and ask the owner if they may strip the tree of the mature fruit. Breadfruit is something of an acquired taste, and the owner is usually delighted. Breadfruit is never eaten raw but baked, steamed or boiled and fried—the riper the better.

BANANA trees are tolerated or hidden in many private gardens as they can look awfully shaggy. However, there is something gratifying about chopping down a stalk with the "hand" (or bunch, which grows upside down) of fruit from your own yard. The whole stump should be cut down, and soon thereafter a new shoot appears. Once planted, bananas are hard to get rid of. Bluefield, Chinese and Ice Cream are the tastiest and most popular varieties. Early Hawaiians brought this staple from the South Seas. There are two types, the cooking and eating.

Cooking bananas should never be eaten raw. Bananas should be yellow and fully ripe with no trace of green when eaten or cooked, and the fibrous strings removed. Because of their highly nutritious value, mothers start their babies on mashed bananas at a very early age. Children and adults alike love plain sliced bananas with milk and sugar or sliced over dry cereal. Try sliced bananas in pancake batter.

POHAS once grew wild on all the islands but are now becoming scarce and are found mostly on Hawaii and Maui. The fruit is about the size of a small cherry, with waxy orange skin enclosed in a tissue-paper like shell and full of many small seeds. *Poha* jam sells for a pretty price, and understandably so if you pick and make your own.

The MANGO is one of Hawaii's most beautiful trees. Its changing foliage, the different colored and textured leaves, the mass of budding flowers, and the hanging fruit present an ever-changing spectacle. The good old *kamaaina* variety, the common mango, grows to great proportions. (Who, today still eats green mangoes with Hawaiian salt or soy?) The Pirie and Haden mango trees are planted in many gardens for their smaller size and large luscious fruits. For sheer enjoyment wash the ripe fruit, peel the smooth thick skin, eat over the kitchen sink, and let the juice run down your arm. Beware, though. The sugar content adds up to many, many calories!

COCONUTS were brought from the South Seas by the early Hawaiians for food, drink, fiber, oil, and utensils. Not many people seek out the coconut tree to plant in their yards today. Besides the hazard of falling nuts, the idea of disposing of dried leaves and fronds is frightening. (The stripped stiff mid-ribs, *ni-au*, can be tied together for brooms or used to stick flowers on.) The meat of the green coconut has a custardlike consistency and is delectable. Slash the nut in half and eat the meat from the shell with a spoon. The meat of the older coconut is hard and white with lots of water. Husk and poke out the three eyes on top to drain out liquid before cracking in half. Coconuts are sold conveniently husked. Coconut chips and coconut bits are good cocktail snacks. Coconut honey or syrup over waffles or ice cream is nectar. Curry isn't curry without coconut milk (the cream extracted from the grated meat and strained) in the sauce, and grated coconut as one of the condiments.

No one grows PINEAPPLES for pleasure —only on plantations for cans and markets. Don Paulo Marin brought pineapples in 1813, and history repeatedly refers to this fruit as the symbol of hospitality and welcome. To share a precious pineapple with friends was the height of hospitality. The miniature fruit makes perfect shells for fruit cocktail. The mature fruit weighs from five to eight pounds and grows on a low plant resembling a cactus with sharp pointed leaves. It takes eighteen months to mature. Pity the poor *malihini* who goes on a "pineapple jag." The great amount of acid in the fresh pineapple can cause hives and sores in the mouth.

To pare a ripe pineapple you need a sharp knife. Cut off the crown and bottom and slice off rind from top to bottom, remove the eyes by gouging with corer or by cutting grooves around the fruit. Rub it well with Hawaiian salt, rinse, cut in round slices or in long wedges. Store covered in refrigerator. Pineapple slices are a great addition to iced tea. Serve alone with cottage cheese for weight-watcher salad. Substitute small pieces of pineapple (no core) for mangoes and make pineapple chutney.

PAPAYA trees are grown commercially in the rurual areas, but once in a while a 'topsy' grows in the garden and bears fruit—if not proven to be a male tree! The Solo type is most popular—no cross-pollenization necessary. The meat varies from pale yellow to salmon-pink and even a watermelon red. The milk can cause irritation to hands and eyes. Many Islanders have this fruit every morning at breakfast—cold with a slice of lemon or lime. It is a perfect base for fruit salads and cocktails. Not recommended for freezing.

Today GUAVAS are hard to come by. Wild guavas are much smaller than the relatively new cultivated ones. Inside coloring ranges from white to yellow to pink to red with a thick yellow shell when ripe. Guava fights were a part of our childhood—nice, squashy over-ripe ones were the best to throw. Who, born of the Islands, can ever forget the scent of guava and ginger—and occasionally horse! Those old days of hiking or riding up into the mountains for guavas and finding a mountain stream to cool off! Summer time was and still is guava time. If you pick too many, you can throw them in the freezer in a plastic bag. Try to pick mostly half-ripe fruit as they are the best for preserves.

The STRAWBERRY GUAVA is quite different. This tree grows wild and tall in mountain areas, but landscape artists use the tree in many gardens for its "prunable" shape, shiny bark and green leaves, rather than for its small sweet fruit. Strawberry guavas have a more acid flavor than regular guavas, and taste luscious eaten dead ripe from the tree or made into jelly.

LILIKOI, PASSION FRUIT OR WATER LEMON vines can still be found growing rampant in most any overgrown area. Passion fruit is the sour yellow-skinned variety and the *lilikoi* is sweet and purple. The shell of the fruit is quite hard, brittle, and shiny, and the inner white pulp serves as a sac for the many small black seeds and very acid juice. To make the basic juice squeeze seeds and juice through several thicknesses of cheesecloth and refrigerate. This does make jelly but needs pectin and tends to be runny. Fresh passion fruit juice is excellent. To freeze: pour juice into ice trays, empty into sacks when frozen and keep in freezer for future use.

The SOURSOP is the "conversation piece" of Hawaiian fruits. People always stop to look at the small evergreen tree with its strange looking fruit. Kidney or heart shaped, with a thick, dark green skin covered with tiny horns or fleshy spines, it measures six to eight inches long and weighs from one to five pounds. The white pulp with many black seeds has the combined flavor of mango and pineapple. It makes excellent sherbet, and may be eaten raw when ripe. The juice is extracted by putting the pulp through a ricer or food mill.

There are PLUMS grown in Hawaii but always in higher elevations. The ripe fruit is small and sweet, but mainland plums are more popular in the markets.

AVOCADO or ALLIGATOR PEAR abounds in calories with its high oil content. Used mostly for salads or soups; some prefer eating it from the half shell with salt and pepper, catsup, French dressing, or even sugar. It does not freeze well and tends to become watery when thawed. A squirt of lemon or lime over cut avocado keeps it from turning black.

WATERMELON, the luscious fruit of sweetness and juice. During the peak summer months the rural roads are dotted with trucks and stands selling the fruit. Always serve it cold whether in salads, fruit cups or plain. Watermelon balls are so much prettier than plain old cubes.

The SURINAM CHERRY is a feathery-leafed tree, but the landscape artists love to clip them as hedges or decorative shrubs. The fruit is small, ribbed and color stages vary from green to bright orange, bright red and very dark ruby red when fully ripe. The fruit is high in acid and popular for preserves.

CARAMBOLA was always called the star

fruit because of its star shape when cut in half. The yellow fruit can be eaten raw and has a wild flavor. In November and December they fall by the buckets and make perfect Thanksgiving and Christmas fruit arrangements.

CARISSA, a thorny shrub with dark green leaves, white flowers and bright red fruit makes a good hedge. It is a relatively new plant to the Islands. A large green branch with red berries makes appropriate Christmas decorations. When the berries fall, just stick small red apples on the thorns. You can use small branches for centerpieces and stick flowers on the thorns. It takes lots of sugar and pectin to make jelly from the fruit.

LYCHEES originally came to Hawaii dried and packed in a fancy colorful Chinese box for Christmas presents. What a mess those crinkly, crackly shells and hard pits made. Only recently were the trees introduced to the Islands. When the fruit is ripening and the branches are pregnant and groaning with bunches of the red fruit, the proud owner suddenly finds he has many, many friends. However, this friendship is short-lived as the season is June and July and one year you may have a bumper crop and the next nil. Some sell their tree to a supplier who strips the ripe fruit and leaves the owner a few fruit with no work. Lychees are sold in bunches and bring a fancy price at market. If, by any chance, you find yourself with an over-abundance, you can freeze them in a cellophane bag—branch, leaves, fruit and

all. But if you insist on stripping them, leave a good two inches of stem on the fruit so that the flesh is not exposed. Fresh lychees are sweet and juicy and a great addition to fresh fruit salad or cocktail when shelled and pitted. Canned lychees from the Orient are delicious in their own syrup.

There are several kinds of CITRUS FRUITS in the Islands. The LIME tree is the most popular garden variety as it always is in season and readily available for table use.

KONA ORANGES grow only on Hawaii and are sold in the markets during the holiday season. They have a thin skin and are consumed mostly for juice.

Hawaiian TANGERINES are sweet and produce abundantly during the holiday season, too, which makes them great assets in fruit arrangements. Found in many private gardens, especially in the valleys.

The POMELO or GRAPEFRUIT tree in full fruit would appear to be sagging under the heavy crop. (The fruit would appear to be growing like Siamese twins.) Originally brought to the Islands in 1800, this fruit has always been popular in *kamaaina* gardens. The pomelo should be picked mature and left on the shelf to "mellow" for a week or two.

The CALAMONDIN (*ALANI-AWA-AWA*) is sometimes referred to as the Chinese orange. The tree is small and when in fruit is studded with small (1″ diameter) oranges. Terribly sour, they are good only for preserves.

The SEAGRAPE grows mostly along the beaches, and if left to grow wild it can become quite tall. The fruit hangs in clusters of green fruit just as the name would indicate—grapes. During the last world war Admiral Chester Nimitz is said to have introduced the ladies to making jelly from the grapes.

Preserves

BE SURE TO STERILIZE all bottles before jarring. The two cup variety is the most convenient, and the wider the mouth the easier the pouring.

More and more people are coming around to using Haden mangoes instead of the old common mangoes for chutney. Many of the "die-hard" *kamaaina* cooks swear by them now as it takes few of these larger mangoes (2 huge Hadens make 4 C) which means less peeling and slicing.

Old recipes refer to jelly bags but today's household seems to lack such niceties. Several thicknesses of cheesecloth do very nicely. Just tie with string, hang, and simply toss out when finished.

Jam making is more difficult than jelly as the bubbling process can be rather messy and conducive to burns. When making jam it is wise to wrap a clean dish towel around your stirring arm. Those "sputter" burns can be painful. A good precaution is to use a cover, too.

To melt parawax: wash a wide-mouth can thoroughly, dry, and squeeze to form a spout leaving enough room to slip in the sticks of wax. Set over low heat to melt, but be very careful not to let wax drip in heating coils or flame as it can ignite very quickly.

Pineapples are available all year round so can be made up at any time. Because of the acid, be sure your hands are free of cuts, or wear gloves.

Pickled Haden Mango

Boil together for five to ten minutes 1½ C vinegar, 3 C sugar, 1 t whole cloves and 1 stick cinnamon broken in half. When boiling hard, add 2 qts. sliced half-ripe mangoes, bring to boil, turn down to gentle boil for 20 minutes, remove cinnamon, and jar immediately. Good with cold meat or just nibble and enjoy.

Pickled Mangoes

Wash and slice half-green, tender, common mangoes to measure a gallon, add ¾ C Hawaiian salt, and let stand. Meanwhile mix and boil 4 C water, 4 C brown raw sugar, 1½ C vinegar and 2 T red coloring. When cool, add mangoes and jar.

Mango Chutney

There are many MANGO CHUTNEY recipes and each person swears by his so it's all a matter of choice and time involved. It's simple if you don't tackle crates at a time and stagger the peeling and slicing with the cooking. Some girls have solved the boring process of peeling and slicing, chopping and grating by bringing all their equipment and ingredients to a friend's pool and working together in a convivial "chutney bee." Before they know it it's time to go home to pot!

Wash, peel, and slice about 50 common mangoes and sprinkle generously with Hawaiian salt and let stand for three hours at least. In a huge pot boil 5 lbs. sugar and 1 qt. vinegar until syrupy. Drain ½ of sliced mangoes and add to syrup. Cook for about 30 minutes. Add the rest of the drained mangoes and the following: 3 large onions, chopped; 6 cloves garlic, chopped; ½ C fresh ginger, grated and finely sliced; 1 7-oz. jar preserved ginger, sliced plus the juice; 2 1-lb. packages glazed cake mix for fruit cakes; 1 #303 can apricots, pitted; 1 15-oz. box seedless raisins; 4 T salt; 1 t each ginger, cinnamon, and allspice. Stir and keep cooking over even heat for about an hour to an hour and a half, but be sure the bottom is not burning or sticking. The addition of chili peppers is up to the individual. Either put 6 (or more) red peppers in a bag and hang in pot or cut up in small pieces and toss in. However, be careful how you handle those hot peppers— they can burn your fingers and the fumes or juice in the eyes is very unpleasant.

The original recipe called for chopping 1 lb. currants, 1 lb. seeded raisins, ½ lb. blanched almonds, ½ C citron, 1 pkg. lemon peel, 1 pkg. orange peel and soaking the dried apricots, but the candied mix is so much easier!

Mango Chutney

7½ lbs. green mangoes (after slicing); 3 lbs. brown sugar (2 dark, 1 light); 1 lb. raisins; 1 lb. currants; ¼ lb. fresh ginger; 1 large onion; ¼ lb. garlic, 18–20 chili peppers; 1 pt. vinegar; ¼ C (scant) salt. Put peeled garlic, peppers, onion, and ginger through grinder. In a large pot combine all ingredients and boil slowly for 1½ hours to 2 hours after it has started boiling. Jar.

Guava Jelly

After the big guava-picking excursion you're probably exhausted so don't try to tackle all in one day...do the first step. Rinse the fruit, remove blossom end, cut in quarters, and place in that famous old, big pot with just enough water to barely cover guavas. Bring to boil, turn down heat and simmer until fruit is very soft..about ½ hour. Don't bag too much cooked pulp as it drips faster with less, and for clear jelly don't squeeze the bag.

Now the problem is where to place those "bags" so they can drip into a large bowl overnight! The old broom handle solves this nicely. Suspend handle over the backs of two chairs, tie bags securely and leave to drip over the bowls placed on newspaper to save the floor. Of course, if you have dogs, be sure they're kept outside or in the parlor!

Next day you are ready to amalgamate all the clear juice and begin the jelly! It is truly worth the effort to make only 2 C of juice at a time in a shallow pot. The shorter the cooking, the quicker the evaporation and the better the jelly. Boil the juice alone for at least ten minutes and give it a good rolling boil, then add 1 C of sugar for 1 C of juice. Stir and let the mixture roll in a good boil. Watch constantly. When the scum forms, skim but don't ever throw it away..yummy to eat like candy or over ice cream. Test often by dropping from spoon. When three or four drops run together on the spoon and sheet off away from the spoon it's done. Bottle, pour parawax over, and admire your gorgeous work.

Now if you're exhausted from standing over the hot stove, just put the remains of the pulp in the ice box and make the jam later.. don't kill yourself.

Guava Jam

Once your strength (and enthusiasm) is restored put the pulp through a ricer or sieve, small quantities at a time. You'll want to chuck the whole mess, but go on. Into the flat, large pot put the puree and sugar cup for cup, about 4 C each. Bring to boil and once it begins to sputter, turn down the heat, cover and keep stirring until it thickens and sheets from spoon, then bottle. For a little spice you can add some grated ginger and lemon juice, or cinnamon, allspice or mace.

Guava-Pineapple Marmalade

Wash guavas, remove stem and blossom ends, cut in half, remove pulp and seeds (use for jam), cut shells into strips about ⅓" wide to make 4 C. Cover the strips with 3½ C sugar, add 1 C water and let stand 3 to 4 hours. Add 1 t finely chopped ginger, 3½ T lime or lemon juice and 2 C fresh pineapple cut fine. Boil until syrup thickens. Pour and seal.

Pineapple-Papaya-Ginger Marmalade

Sometimes papaya seems rather bland alone and should be zipped up with a sister fruit for dash, and this is the answer. In your large jam pot put 2 C shredded fresh pineapple, 2 C diced fresh, firm papaya, 4 C sugar, 4 t grated fresh ginger and cook to a rolling boil, then turn down the heat and cook until thick, stirring all the while. Bottle immediately when thick and not too runny.

Pineapple Pickle

This is Hawaii's contribution to cold meats. Take 3 firm, large pineapples, peel, cut out eyes, cut crosswise in 1″ thick slices, remove core and cut into sections about 1″ wide. In your favorite pot combine 3 C vinegar, 3½ C water, 2 T whole cloves, 2 sticks cinnamon, and boil for 10 minutes. Add 12 C pineapple sections and boil gently, with cover on, for 45 minutes. For another 20–30 minutes bubble slowly and when the fruit is tender pour into sterilized jars.

Pineapple Jam

Combine 12 C chopped or grated fresh pineapple (no core) and 6 C sugar, and let stand overnight. Next day put in large pot, add 6 T lemon juice and rind of 3 lemons sliced in minute strips. Cook slowly for 2 hours.. stir, stir, stir, stir, stir..test and jar! Remember and watch the bubbly spurts.

Carissa Jelly

Worth making if just for the gorgeous color. Tart, beautiful crimson color and better for cold meats than biscuits. Wash and drain 4 C sliced ripe carissa, add 2 C water and bring to boil and simmer until fruit is tender (15–20 min.). Drip-drain through jelly bag. Bring juice to rolling boil, add sugar (cup for cup) and boil until it sheets from spoon. Jar.

Poha Jam

Husk and wash 4 qts. pohas (if you're so lucky) and cook slowly with little water for 30 minutes. Let stand overnight. For cup of pulp and juice add cup of sugar and squeeze of lemon. Cook slowly over low fire and stir frequently. Fifty minutes should produce signs of thickening. Bottle and don't expect it to last.

Surinam Cherry Jelly

For basic juice wash 5 lbs. ripe cherries, remove stems and blossom ends, add water to barely cover, mash down and around and boil gently for about ½ hour. Pour into the JB to drip away. For the jelly boil 4 C of juice for 10 minutes, add 4 C sugar, bring to boil, and let her roll for about 15 minutes, or until it jells and sheets from spoon. Jar!

Passion Fruit Jelly

Take 3 C freshly squeezed juice and add 1 C of water and 7½ C sugar. Bring to rolling boil and stir. Add 6-oz. bottle of liquid fruit pectin, bring to boil, and quick-rolling boil for 1 minute, stirring all the while. Skim and jar.

Banana Marmalade

Simple and an exciting discovery. Not only

is it tasty but you may use it with toast, for cakes, or cold meats. Slice 10 medium-size bananas into earthenware bowl and sprinkle with juice of one or two lemons (depending on sweetness). Add 3 C granulated sugar, stir and let stand for 1 hour. Pour into jam-making pot and bring to a boil. Turn down heat and keep stirring while it bubbles gently. It should thicken in about 20 minutes and test by dropping by small spoonfuls on plate. Jar.

Coconut Candy

This used to be the pièce de résistance of many of Hawaii's famous cooks and hostesses and was given as gifts or contributions to church bazaars. Today no one really wants to husk, crack, and shred the coconut. However, the freshly grated coconut is the secret to good coconut candy. To shred fresh coconut you sit on and straddle a small piece of board with a projecting head of blades which protrudes over the seat in order for the meat to fall into a bowl beneath. Holding a half of a coconut with two hands, bear down and grate with an up and down motion, careful to stop if the slightest black shows in the pristine white meat. Another way is to scoop the white meat from the shell, cut off the black skin, and grate. But then there always seem to be drops of blood on the pure white. Bring to a rolling boil 3 C of sugar and 1½ C water, pinch of salt, and drop of vanilla. When it is really syrupy add 1 grated coconut and cook until thick, about 10 minutes.

Then beat while hot (like fudge) until creamy. Beware the sugary batter. Drop by spoonfuls on waxed paper. A drop of pink or green coloring adds a pretty touch.

Coconut Candy

Mix 3 C fresh-grated coconut, 3 C sugar, pinch of salt, ½ C milk, and mix thoroughly. On a low fire, bring to a boil, cook 20–30 minutes and beat until creamy. Boiling too long makes candy separate. Drop from teaspoons on wax paper.

Coconut Milk

It is so convenient to buy frozen coconut milk for cooking. However, if you prefer to make your own, grate 4 coconuts. Pour 1 qt. of milk over this and heat thoroughly. Squeeze while hot through canvas or straining cloth and use as a regular cream. You can make it thick or thin as you desire by addition of milk. Use cow's milk, and note that it takes muscles to drain out all the liquid!

"TETTA" (MRS. THOMAS) RICHERT wears many hats: boat and car racing, artist, creative designer, and chef. The following four recipes are proof of her talent in the kitchen.

Calamondin or Alani 'Awa' Awa Jam

Cut the fruit in half, pick out seeds, put into blender, and turn on "grate" until cut into small pieces. (Do not make into mush.) Cook for about 10 minutes, stirring constantly, and let it stand in refrigerator all night. Next day, measure sugar, cup for cup, and cook again until it sheets from spoon. Pour into jars and seal.

Surinam Cherry Jelly

Boil gently 2 C washed surinam cherries in enough water to see through the fruit (about 1 C) for about 8 minutes. Drain through a strainer, allowing some of the pulp to go through in the juice. Measure and then add an equal amount of sugar and the juice of ½ lemon. Boil over high heat in a large pan and stir constantly until jelly sheets from a spoon. Skim and pour into jars. To seal, grate paraffin on top of hot jelly; it will melt and seal. (How now! Great!)

Extra Special Guava Jam

Halve guavas and scoop out seeds. Cut shells, not too fine, in about eighths. To 1 qt. shells, add 1 qt. sugar and let stand overnight. Cook 20 minutes over medium heat. Cook seeds and pulp about 20 minutes, stir, put through strainer. Measure 4 C puree and 3 C sugar.

Add to guava shells and cook (stirring all the time) until it sheets from spoon. Skim and jar.

Seagrape Jelly

To prepare juice: Wash and remove stems of 4 C half-ripe seagrapes, crush in a pan and add ½ C water. Bring to a boil and simmer covered for about 10 minutes. Strain. To 4 C seagrape juice, add 7 C sugar and if juice seems of a mild flavor add ½ C lemon juice. Boil quickly to a full rolling boil that cannot be stirred down, add half of a 6-oz. bottle liquid fruit pectin and bring again to rolling boil for 1 minute. Remove from heat, skim, and pour immediately in jars and seal.

Mango Chutney

KINAU WILDER prefaced this recipe with an emphatic, "Best chutney you ever made!" It was the favorite recipe of her dear friend, the late PEGGY (MRS. DOUGLAS) BLYTHE.

24 C sliced mangoes (2 huge green Haden mangoes make 4 C), 5 lbs. mill sugar (the light brown package which comes in 4 lb. bags), 1 1-lb. box seedless raisins, 1 handful rock salt, 1 whole head garlic, 1 qt. vinegar, 15 chili pepper (or 4 large), and a hand of ginger or 6 pieces the size of your thumb. Now simply put vinegar, chilis, garlic, and ginger in blender to chop up the easy way and add 1 t cinnamon, 1 t nutmeg, 1 t all-spice, 1 t cloves, 1 T mustard seed, 3 finely

sliced lemons with seeds removed. And here is the great part! Combine everything and put whole thing in uncovered roasting pan in 375 F oven and cook 3 hours, stirring occasionally. Makes 10 pts. of the BEST CHUTNEY YOU EVER MADE!

Pepper Pot Jelly

RUTHIE (MRS. L. McCULLY) JUDD, JR. was most emphatic about the peppers in this recipe. It is very important that you clean every trace of seeds from the skin. Then when you hold the finished product to the light it is beautifully clear.

Grind ¼ C red Hawaiian chili peppers (well seeded) and ¾ C bell peppers through the coarse blade. Bring 6½ C white sugar and 1½ C cider vinegar to boil. Remove from stove and let stand for 20 minutes. Stir a little, return to stove, add peppers and bring to full boil for 2 minutes. Remove from stove, skim any foam, add 1 6-oz. bottle liquid fruit pectin, stir 5 minutes, and bottle.

Spiced Figs

MRS. FRANK THOMPSON's gifts of her home-made preserves are a labor of love and treasured by all her friends.

3 lbs. figs, 2½ lbs. sugar, ½ pt. of water, 1 pt. apple cider vinegar, 3 dozen cloves, 4 sticks of cinnamon. Melt sugar in the vinegar and water. When hot, pour over figs and add spices tied in a bag. Let stand 24 hours. Drain syrup off of figs, bring to a boil, then add figs with bag of spices and cook until figs are tender. When you put the hot fruit in sterilized jars, add a stick of cinnamon and a few of the spices to each jar. Seal very tight. Put aside for 6 months. (Use white figs.)

Kukui Nut (Inamona)

LAMBERT APO prefers to make his own *kukui* nut and it all sounded too easy.

Roast the whole kukui nut slowly in the oven for about an hour or until brown, crack with hammer, and remove the kernel of meat. Then pound, NOT CHOP, with rock or handle of knife or blunt end of something, add a pinch of Hawaiian salt, fry it in pan a few minutes, and bottle.

Mango Chutney

CHARLES ROBINSON, interior decorator-artist, has a great *joie de vivre* and a flair for the humorous. His kitchen is a work shop for creating delectable Island fruit recipes and other goodies. Charlie emphatically says: "Use *only* common mangoes for chutney *unless*, of course, you want mush!" (Another *kamaaina* view on the mango-for-chutney saga.)

50 green common mangoes; 1 lb. white Hawaiian salt; ½ C chopped fresh ginger; 2 large onions, chopped; 2 small cloves garlic; 1 15-oz. box seedless raisins; 1 11-oz. box currants; 6 lbs. brown sugar; 2½ qts, cider vinegar; ¼ C chopped Hawaiian chili peppers; 3 t nutmeg; 3 t ground cloves; 3 t ground ginger; 6 t allspice; nuts optional.

Peel and slice mangoes, cover with Hawaiian salt (no water) in stonewear basin and let stand overnight. Drain mangoes, wash and squeeze slices as dry as possible. Put in large enamel pot and add all spices, sugar and vinegar, chopped chili peppers, chopped onions, raisins, and currants. Tie chopped ginger and halved garlic cloves in cheese-cloth bags and drop in pot. Bring to boil, reduce heat to medium and cook for 2½ hours stirring often. Pour into sterilized hot jars and cover with paraffin and seal.

Keeps for years and improves with age. If mold appears, open jars and remove paraffin and mold and reboil chutney for a few minutes, re-bottle, and cover with new paraffin and seal. If added spices are desired this procedure may be used to achieve desired taste. Makes 12 pints.

Pineapple Pickle

Charlie's pineapple pickle secret is the little Hawaiian chili pepper.

9 lbs. (6) fresh pineapple; 5 lbs. brown sugar: 5½ C cider vinegar; 4 heaping T pickling spices; 6 cinnamon sticks, crushed; fresh Hawaiian red chili peppers. Peel, pare, and cut pineapple into chunks. Place in large enamel pot and add all ingredients except chili pepper. Bring to boil and reduce heat to slow boil for 1 hour or longer until fruit is tender and translucent in appearance. Put in sterilized jars and add enough liquid to cover fruit and then place one whole fresh red chili pepper in each jar. Paraffin, seal, and cap. Let stand for at least 30 days before serving.

Calamondin Preserve

CHARLES ROBINSON experimented with the small Calamondin orange and came up with a superb relish to serve with any fowl, and especially good with pork or venison. The left-over juice from the preserves he bottles and uses to glaze his baked hams. Good over ice cream, too.

Wash about 90 small oranges and cut stem to stern. (He doesn't bother with the seeds then as he likened it to dissecting a grasshopper!) Cover with water in saucepan and simmer covered until tender, a little more than half hour. (It is during this simmering that he sits with a slotted spoon and picks out the many seeds.) Drain. Boil 4 C sugar, 1 C vinegar, ½ C water, 10 whole cloves, 2 cinnamon sticks for 5 minutes, add cooked oranges, and simmer until they are well glazed. Pack oranges in sterilized jars, add 1 chili pepper (optional) to each jar and fill with the syrup. Cool and seal with paraffin.

Yvonne (Mrs. John) Armitage takes great pride and time in her art of cooking and her following three preserve recipes are outstanding.

Dilled Crisscross Carrots

2 lbs. carrots, 1 ⅓ C white vinegar, 1 ⅓ C water, ½ t each celery seed, mustard seed, caraway seed, 1½ t dill seed, 1 C sugar, 1 t Hawaiian salt and ½ t crushed Hawaiian red peppers. Wash, scrape, and cut carrots into thin crisscross slices, using special corrugated slicer available at most kitchen cutlery counters in stores locally. Cook carrots in a very little salted water until almost tender. Pack them closely into hot sterilized pint jars. Make syrup of remaining ingredients. Bring them to a full rolling boil, boil for 2 minutes, then pour syrup over carrots to overflowing and seal tightly with jar covers. Makes 4 pints.

Dell's Pineapple Pickles

6 C fresh pineapple, cut into medium chunks; 2 C sugar; 1 C cider vinegar; 12 whole cloves; 6 2″ sticks cinnamon. Put all ingredients into good sized sauce pan, bring to boil, turn heat to medium and cook until pineapple looks clear. Pour fruit and syrup into hot sterilized jars and seal tightly. Let jars "ripen" a few weeks before using, to let fruit absorb spices.

Surinam Cherry Sauce

6 C cherries, 1 C water, 4¼ to 4½ C sugar. Wash the cherries in a sink full of water, removing blossom ends. Put cherries in large pot, add water, and boil slowly until the cherries are quite soft. Press them through a sieve to remove the seeds. Return pulp to pot, measuring amount first. Add sugar, cup for cup, and bring pulp quickly to a boil, and continue boiling until it thickens. Pour into hot sterilized jars and seal immediately with clean jar covers. This sauce is a wonderful meat condiment and is especially good with lamb.

Mixed Pickles

Shada (Mrs. Ed) Bryan's closets are filled with her homemade preserves. This is one of her more different recipes.

4 C cucumber pieces, 2 C carrot pieces, 1 cauliflower, 2 sweet red peppers, 2 C pickling onions, 1¼ qt. vinegar, 1½ t tumeric, 5 C sugar, 3 (4 oz.) cans mushrooms, 1 C salt, 1 gal. water, 4 T mustard seed, 3 T celery seed, ¼ qt. water, 1 T pickling spice (remove pieces of pepper).

Wash, rinse, and drain vegetables before measuring. Quarter cucumbers and cut into 1″ lengths. Cut carrots into ½″ pieces; measure. Break cauliflower into small flowerlets. Seed and chop peppers; peel onions. Drain mushrooms. Put all the vegetables in a stone crock. Dissolve salt in water; pour over vegetables. Let stand 18 hours, drain. Combine sugar, vinegar, mustard seed, celery seed, crushed red pepper, and pickling spice; boil 3 minutes Add vegetables, simmer until thoroughly heated, then bring to a rolling boil, and pack boiling hot into hot jars.

Pickled Onions

JACK (MR. JOHN C.) WALKER has another Maui winner!

Peel 3 lbs. small white Maui onions. Soak in plenty of Hawaiian salt and water overnight. Next day drain well. Put in large pot: 1 qt. white vinegar, 4 C white sugar, 2 T salt, 1 T more or less mustard seed and the following, which are optional, should be bagged: 1 t each of allspice, cinnamon, cloves, nutmeg. Bring to a boil, cool, and pour over onions and bottle.

MAE (MRS. GOODALE) MOIR is THE fountain of knowledge when it comes to preserves and canning, and rightfully so! She turned an old plantation 3-bedroom home into a jelly factory before World War II and worked by trial and error and learned the hard way. Her preserves were sold under the brand name of HAWAIIAN MAID PRESERVES.

She passed along two tips which are invaluable. When making papaya chutney use apricot color but hard papayas. As you peel and dice them plunge the pieces in a pan of cold water and this pulls out the milk.
When making chutney, plop fruit into the boiling syrup and boil until the fruit is translucent. Turn off the fire and leave on the back of the stove. Next day bring to boil and bottle.

Tamarind Syrup

This is Mae's basic recipe for drinks or to add to her chutney recipe. For tamarind ade, water down with water or soda and add sugar to taste.
3½ lbs. shelled tamarinds. Cover with water and let stand until absorbed. Cover again and let stand overnight. Cook with water for 20 minutes. Strain through coarse sieve, put seeds on to boil again with water, and strain again. Boil all syrup together with 5 lbs. brown sugar and extra water if needed, and boil 10 minutes. Bottle.

Tamarind-Mango Chutney

Bring to a boil and simmer 5 lbs. sugar; 1 qt. vinegar; 1 qt. tamarind syrup; 1 lb. whole raisins; 1 lb. ground raisins; ½ lb. currants; 6 chopped chili peppers; 3 fingers ginger cut in narrow strips; salt. Add 13 lbs. sliced mangoes, boil until done. Remember to keep stirring. Jar.

Sweet Mango Pickle

1 large green mango, 1 C brown sugar, ½ C water, ½ C vinegar, 5 cloves, cinnamon, 3 peppercorns, ¼ bay leaf. Make syrup, bring to boil, boil 5 minutes. Add mango slices and cook until tender. Fill tall jars to within 1″ and fill to within ¼″ with plain boiled water, and seal.

Papaya Pickle

Cook syrup of 4 C sugar, 2 C vinegar, 12 cloves, 16 peppercorns, 4 bay leaves and simmer for ½ hour. Put aside. Cook 8 C half-ripe papaya in 2 C water until tender, drain off water, add to syrup, bring to boil, and bottle.

Papaya Chutney

Boil 2¼ C vinegar, and 3½ C raw sugar for a few minutes. Add 2 T chopped ginger; 3 seeded chili peppers chopped fine; 1 clove garlic chopped; and 1¼ t salt and cook a little longer. Add 14 C cubed half-ripe, firm papayas and 3 C seedless raisins. Cook until mixture thickens to desired consistency. Be careful of the sticky bottom! Jar and seal.

Mango Jelly

Peel and slice green, full-grown mangoes. Cover fruit with water and let stand in porcelain kettle overnight. Boil 20 minutes. Drain off liquid and put right on stove again to boil. In 10 minutes put in equal parts of sugar and boil 20–30 minutes until it jells. Use pulp for jam.

Chinese Orange Marmalade

Cut oranges in half, squeeze out juice and seeds and strain. Take skins and put through medium grind, combine juice and ground skin, add 1 C water to gallon of mixture. Bring to boil and remove (sticks easily) from fire. Measure pulp and add sugar, cup for cup. It jells very rapidly, so stir constantly and be ready as soon as it comes to boil because it will give the jelly test almost immediately. Jar. Mae uses this marmalade for several dishes: adds it to lemon chiffon pie, spreads it on baking bananas, and glazes her pork chops which she grills *after* slipping them into boiling water for 15 minutes!

Spiced Grapes

The late Mrs. Robert A. Catton's home in Nuuanu Valley is one of the remaining old-style *kamaaina* homes—wide lanais, hanging baskets, potted plants, and in the back yard well-tended grape vines. This is her very own recipe for the grapes they don't eat.

Wash and stem 7 lbs. Isabella grapes and remove skins (keep skins). Cook pulp until soft enough to put through fine strainer. Add skins, 5 lbs. sugar, 1 pint cider vinegar, 1 t cloves, 2½ t allspice, 2½ t cinnamon and cook slowly for 1½ hours. Put in jars and seal while hot. Excellent with cold meats.

DESSERTS

AN ELDERLY HAWAIIAN LADY said to me recently, "When I was a child our dessert was fresh bread and butter with homemade guava jelly or jam or lots of fresh fruit." A sweet tooth pleaser and "strengthener" was the freshly peeled sugar cane. As a matter of fact, a small clump of sugar cane waved in many a garden.

Then there was Miss Emily Ladd's fresh coconut cake for special occasions and those cans of sweetened condensed milk to spread on saloon pilots—or saloon pilots soaked in coffee, milk and sugar, removed to the saucer, and doused with butter.

The good old homemade cakes of the past are mostly memories now. Occasionally at a church fair or special occasion you can find homemade prune, tomato, coconut, or chocolate cakes that absolutely melt in the mouth, but on the whole bakeries thrive—not to mention the package mixes!

Honolulu hostesses are keen on fruits, sherbets, and ices and prefer to serve these lighter desserts, especially in hot weather.

Banana Cake

This moist cake needs no frosting and can be served alone or with fresh fruit, and either hot or cold. Cream ½ lb. butter with 2 C sugar, when frothy add 4 eggs, 1 t vanilla and beat. Add 2 C blended banana alternately with 2½ C flour sifted with 2 t soda (you'll be sorry if soda lumps taste bitter in the cake) and 1 t salt. Bake in loaf pan at 350 for 1 hour or until cake rises and pulls away from the pan. The runny liquid of the blended banana takes the place of milk. Wrapped properly these cakes freeze very well.

Bananas au Rum

Peel bananas and cut in half lengthwise, place in greased pan and sprinkle with lime juice, dribble honey over, and pour on the rum. Bake and baste for 20 minutes at 250 F and broil to brown. Naturally, add more rum with whipped cream when serving.

Baked Bananas and Coconut Cream

Peel 8 bananas, place in buttered pan, and dribble over 1 C of honey. Bake in hot oven until brown and puffed. Serve hot with coconut cream.

Mango Bread

Very much like banana bread and excellent plain. Cream ½ C shortening, ¾ C sugar until fluffy, add 3 beaten eggs and mix well. Add alternately 3 C flour sifted with 1 t soda and ¼ t salt with 1 C of mashed ripe mangoes sprinkled with 1 T lemon juice. ½ C chopped macadamia nuts optional. Bake 1 hour in loaf pan at 375 F.

Mango Pie

You could follow your favorite apple pie recipe and substitute the mangoes for apples. Line a pie pan with pastry, put in a good layer of half ripe mangoes, sprinkle with mixture of: 1½ C sugar, cinnamon, nutmeg, lemon juice, 3 T flour and 2–3 t water. Cover with more sliced mangoes and spice mixture. Cover with pastry, poke holes with fork and bake in 425 F oven for 10 minutes, then reduce to 350 F for about 40 minutes. Serve hot with whipped cream—gorgeous!

Soursop Sherbet

Simple to make and has a piquant flavor. Boil 2 C water and 7/8 C sugar for about 10 minutes to make syrup, cool to lukewarm, and add 2 C soursop puree (put fruit through ricer or sieve), 1 T lemon juice and 1 unbeaten egg white. Mix and pour into freezing tray.

Soursop Mousse

This may take a little more time but is tastier. Add 2 T sugar and 20 marshmallows to ¼ C water. Heat slowly until marshmallows are soft and the mixture is smooth. When cool, add 1 C soursop puree and let stand until partially congealed. Add 1 C whipped cream, pour into mold and freeze.

Coconut Dessert

Beat 1 pt. whipping cream until stiff and add 1 t vanilla. Dissolve 2 ¼-oz. packages of gelatin in 2 T water and add to cream. Mix well and then add half a fresh coconut grated. Spoon into Pyrex dish and place in refrigerator for 3 hours or more. Serve with cold sliced mangoes, peaches, strawberries, or grapes and sprinkle grated coconut from the other half of nut over all.

Coconut Shortbread Cookies

Forget about calories and let these melt in the mouth. Cream 1 C butter (oleo only if you must) with 3 T sugar, add 2 C sifted flour, 1 C grated fresh coconut and 1 t vanilla. Form into rolls like icebox cookies, wrap and chill. Slice ¼″ thick and bake 30–35 minutes at 300 on ungreased cookie sheet. Remove from pan while warm and sprinkle with sifted powdered sugar until fully coated.

Mango Sauce

Use half-ripe fruit on the tart side. Cook until tender and not too mushy 6 C sliced mangoes, 1½ C water, and 1 to 2 C sugar, depending on tartness of fruit. Can be served plain, with heavy cream, over ice cream or in a tart shell with whipped cream. Mangoes substitute beautifully for pineapple in upside down cake or Brown Betty.

Pineapple Compote

Combine cubed fresh pineapple, pitted fresh lychees and green and red maraschino cherries and marinate in rum. Serve cold and garnish with fresh sprigs of mint.

Minted Pineapple

An excellent luncheon dessert. Cut a fresh pineapple lengthwise or in cubes and place in large crock or jar. Pour over a simple syrup of sugar and water and lots of chopped fresh mint. This should stand in the refrigerator to mellow and be served cold.

Lychees in Kirsch

Serve fresh, pitted lychees, very cold, swimming in kirsch.

Fresh Fruit on Bamboo Sticks

If you're serving a heavy meal, fruit with a choice of cheese makes an excellent dessert. Cut watermelon, mango, papaya, or any other colorful fruit in season into bite size cubes and thread on the bamboo sticks.

Miscellaneous

Chinese rice puffs and fortune cookies (sembei) which come packaged in cellophane bags at the market are marvelous to serve with fresh fruit.

* * * * *

After an oriental dinner, serve Chinese preserved candy—colorful and delicious for a change. Candied ginger, carrots, watermelon, and coconut are the most popular and can be bought at a chop suey house.

Hawaiian Angel Food Cake

OLLIE (MRS. R. L.) MILLER conceived this dessert especially for visiting relatives from the mainland and now graciously shares it. She calls it, appropriately enough, "Eat and Drink."

With a fork tear fresh angel food cake into serving pieces, saturate with sauterne until it is literally soaked, then refrigerate. Before serving, put cake on individual dessert plates, pour sour cream or plain yogurt over to cover, and top with slices of a good sweet papaya or mango for taste and color. Sprinkle crushed macadamia nuts over all.

Pumpkin Pie

Ollie suggests that the next time you make your favorite pumpkin pie try substituting coconut milk for regular milk and use some freshly grated coconut sparingly. Surprise!

Grape Pie

"TETTA" (MRS. THOMAS) RICHERT is sure her mother invented this pie—she remembers her saying: "If you can make a raisin pie, why not use grapes?" "Tetta" has never seen a recipe for this pie nor eaten it anywhere but at home. (Delicious, too!)

Take 4 C of seedless grapes and wash and remove all stems. Mix together in a bowl: 1 C white sugar, ½ C flour, dash of salt, 1 t nutmeg, and pinch of cinnamon. Blend thoroughly and then add the grapes, stirring around until each grape is coated with the sugar-flour mixture.

Line a pie pan with crust (you can buy ready-made pie crust mixes) and sprinkle 1 T of sugar in the bottom. Pour in the coated grapes, spreading the remaining sugar and flour mixture over them. Squeeze half a lemon over this and dot with butter. Add the top crust and seal edges. Make a few cuts in the top crust, brush with milk and sugar lightly, add a dash of nutmeg and put into a preheated 450 F oven for 15 minutes. Reduce heat to 350 F and cook for another 35 minutes or until it looks bubbly and is nicely browned.

Passion Fruit Cake

TETTA RICHERT's love for speed must have conjured up this Hawaiian delight!

Take 1 1-lb. yellow cake mix (packaged), add 1 3-oz. package lemon jello, 1 t vanilla, 3 eggs, ¾ C water, ¾ C cooking oil and mix. Pour into a 9″ × 13″ oblong cake tin and bake at 350 for about 35–45 minutes. Remove from oven, prick entire cake with a large fork, and pour over following mixture while still hot: 1 6-oz. can frozen passion fruit juice (thawed) mixed with ½ lb. of powdered sugar, juice of 2 lemons and 1 small lime, and about ¼ C water. Pour over hot cake evenly, let cool and serve.

Julie (Mrs. Joseph) Palma kindly gave the following delectable desserts which are truly Hawaiian and simple to prepare.

Mangoes and Lychees

Place sliced mangoes (fresh or frozen) and fresh, frozen, or canned lychees in dessert cups and top with a T of pineapple or passion fruit sherbet. Pass kirsch to pour over.

Ginger Sauce

This sauce will keep for months in the refrigerator and is delicious over vanilla ice cream or angel food cake.

1 7-oz. jar of preserved ginger in syrup. Drain ginger, saving the syrup; chop ginger fine in chopping bowl and combine again with syrup. Add maple syrup to taste—about ½ C or more.

Cream Puffs

Either make your own or buy them at your favorite bakery, and use melted guava jelly as a sauce. Put guava jelly in a double boiler and add about ¼ C water for a 2-cup jar jelly.

Mrs. Alice Spalding Bowen is a charming feminine combination of business woman, civic leader, and hostess supreme. Mrs. Bowen is noted for her exquisite detail in table settings and menus fit for a queen—not only delicious but appealingly attractive. The following recipes are recommended for summer desserts.

Champagned Mangoes

Take large Pirie mangoes and cut in half around the circumference, twist free of seed and remove each half intact from the skin. (Only the Pirie can be freed from its seed in this manner.) Put each half in a deep champagne glass and add a scoop of fresh pineapple sherbet. When served at the table, fill the glass immediately with iced champagne.

Summer Luncheon Dessert

Always add to your herb garden a few strawberry plants for their lovely and useful leaves. Make individual ice molds, using all your ingenuity, and freeze within their sides two or three strawberry leaves. Buy from the market those huge imported fresh strawberries to heap in the hollowed center of the ice molds. Pass your antique silver powdered sugar sifter and a pitcher of kirsch and the rare DOLFI wild strawberry liqueur from France.

Compote Flambé

Make a compote of equal parts of sliced marons, kumquats, and Chinese preserved ginger, moistened with the ginger syrup. Pour over the compote "Flambé Fanfare," (Ivaldis brandy flavored extract which "flames foods instantly") and serve it, flaming, in a chaffing dish or silver bowl accompanied with a bowl of vanilla ice cream. (Marons are candied chestnuts preserved in syrup with a vanilla flavor, imported from France. A deluxe touch to gourmet cooking or garnish.)

Melon Bowl

Cut a large sweet watermelon in half. Scoop out the melon in large balls (with ice cream scoop). Clean the melon "bowl" and scallop the edge. When ready to serve, combine melon balls with an equal number of pineapple sherbet balls, filling the bowl.

Around its base arrange a garland of mint. Serve with a pitcher of mixed liqueurs, ⅓ each kirsch, Cointreau and Grand Marnier.

Marmalade Pudding

JACK (MR. JOHN C.) WALKER's mother (Mrs. John S. Walker) was a marvelous cook and he still remembers and covets her famous pudding.

Combine: 1 C chopped suet, 1 C marmalade, 2½ C stale bread crumbs, ½ C milk, 1 egg, and 1 t bicarbonate of soda dissolved in 1 T hot water. Mix altogether and steam in covered tin for 2 hours. Serve with foamy sauce: Cream ½ C butter, 1 C powdered sugar, add beaten egg and 2 T vanilla. Let stand on hot stove but do not boil.

Mini Banana Muffins

"BABY" MAY (MRS. ALEXANDER) ROSS sent this along with the footnote: "This is so easy to make and there are always those old bananas hanging around—busy days I make up the batter and store in refrigerator for a couple of days until I'm ready to bake them, and they freeze beautifully after being baked."

Cream ¼ lb. butter and 1½ C sugar; add 2 eggs, beaten; then 1 C mashed bananas mixed with 2 T lemon juice. Sift 2 C flour, 1 t salt, 1 t baking soda and stir in alternately with ¾ C sour milk. (To sour milk put 1 T vinegar in cup and add milk.) Add 1 t vanilla. Bake at 350 for 20 minutes. Use well greased "mini" muffin pans. Macadamia nuts or walnuts may be chopped and added to the batter. (She doesn't say, "or oleo"!)

MRS. SARAH (JAMES) WILDER served these two favorite desserts at her parties, and the guests always had seconds.

Pineapple Upside-Down Cake

¼ C butter; 1 C brown sugar; 8 slices pineapple well drained; 1½ C sifted flour; 1 C sugar; 2 t baking powder; ½ t salt, ¼ C non-fat dry milk, ½ C shortening, soft; ⅔ C pineapple juice, 1 t vanilla, 2 unbeaten eggs. Melt butter over low heat in skillet. Remove and sprinkle brown sugar over melted butter. Arrange pineapple slices on sugar. Sift flour, sugar, baking powder, salt and non-fat dry milk into a 2 qt. bowl. Add shortening. Stir in half of mixture of juice and vanilla. Beat *hard* 2 minutes with electric mixer, medium speed. Add rest of liquid and the eggs. Beat hard 2 minutes longer. Pour batter over pineapple. Bake on rack slightly below center at 350 F for 45–55 minutes. Let cake stand 5 minutes before turning out.

Guavas in Jelly

1 C guava pulp; 2 ½-oz. pkgs. gelatin; ¾ C sugar; ½ C cold water; 1½ C boiling water. Soak gelatin in cold water for 5 minutes and combine with sugar and guava pulp. Add boiling water, then coloring (only when using white guavas). Pour into cold wet mold and chill. Serve with plain or whipped cream.

LAMBERT APO is a genial custodian during the week, but come the weekend you can find him bending over a hot imu or grating coconuts by the crates for the rich cream to make *haupia*. Here is his recipe for a large quantity (and excellent quality).

Haupia

1 gallon of coconut milk (half water, half coconut cream mixed, because if you used the straight cream it would be too rich. You can use the frozen milk instead of the freshly grated for cream), ¾ of a 1-lb. box of plain cornstarch in the yellow box, and 4 C sugar. Add the sugar gradually to the pot of coconut milk to taste and bring to boil, stirring occasionally with a wooden spoon. Stir in the cornstarch mixed with water and don't stop stirring—about a minute or minute and a half—and test by dropping slowly from spoon for desired thickness. Pour quickly into flat pan and cut when cool. Lambert assured me that it wasn't necessary to refrigerate the *haupia* for at least a day. Once refrigerated, it tends to harden.

DORA (MRS. STEPHEN A.) DERBY is a great believer in freezing guavas for future use.

Freezing Raw Guava Pulp

Add 1 part sugar to 4 or 5 parts guava puree according to taste. Mix thoroughly, package in 2 C containers and freeze. She has learned that if you put the scooped out pulp into the blender for an instant or before it grinds up the seeds, it is much easier to put through sieve.

Freezing Raw Guava Shells

Peel yellow skins, scoop out center (use for jam later), slice rind and combine 1 part sugar and 4 parts guava rind. Put in freezing containers and add 35% sugar syrup to cover the shells. (1 ⅓ C sugar and 2 C water mixed and brought to full rolling boil, then cooled.) Be sure to press down with spoon until all the air bubbles have risen. You can use these for many things. One way is to thaw, drain off syrup, and add rinds to large fruit compote.

Guavas in Jelly

1 C uncooked guava pulp; juice of one lime; 2 ¼-oz. pkgs. gelatin; ¾ C sugar or to taste (if you are using frozen pulp cut down on sugar); ¼ t salt; ½ C cold water; 1½ C boiling water. Soak gelatin in cold water 5 minutes; combine sugar and guava pulp; dissolve gelatin in boiling water, add to guava pulp, stir well, pour into cold wet-ring mold, and chill. When serving fill the center of ring with sliced raw guava rinds sweetened to taste and top with whipped cream.

Guava Mousse

1½ C guava pulp; 1½ C whipping cream; 1 C powdered sugar; ¼ t salt. Whip cream and fold into guava pulp which has been mixed with sugar and salt. Freeze 4 hours in mold. Use sliced guava rind for garnish. Provides 8 servings.

Cooked Guava Shells

Peel rind of ripe or nearly ripe guavas and scoop out seeds and pulp. Cut rind in half and set aside. Put seeds and pulp in pot, cover with water and add sugar to make syrup. Strain and use this liquid to poach halved or quartered guava shells—depending on size of guava. Simmer until tender, cool and freeze. Good on ice cream. Dora says that sweet guavas are not too good—rather 'blah' unless you add lime juice. The good old common sour variety is the best!

Melon Dessert

MAE (MRS. GOODALE) MOIR's artistic touch comes out in this pretty and cool dessert.

In your best silver or Celadon bowl place a red torch ginger bud in the center and around it place green melon balls and then a rim of watermelon balls. You may add sprigs of mint for greenery.

Lime Pie

RUTHIE (MRS. L. McCULLY) JUDD, JR. Highly recommends this dessert as it takes only minutes to prepare and the guests "have to have the recipe"!

Make a graham cracker crust: blend 2 C graham cracker crumbs (store bought), ¾ C sugar, ½ C melted butter and line the pie pan. Reserve a little to sprinkle over top. Bake for only 5–8 minutes at 375 F. Open a can of sweetened condensed milk, beat a ½ pint jar of avoset whipping cream, mix these with ½ C lime juice until well blended and pour into crust. Sprinkle remaining graham cracker mixture on top and leave in refrigerator.

CATHARINE (MRS. REGINALD H.) CARTER always has glass jars or cans filled with delectable homemade cookies in her pantry —a ready treat for young and old.

Date Bars

Beat 3 eggs until light and fluffy, add 1 C sugar, 1 C flour sifted with ½ t salt and 1 t baking powder, and beat until smooth. Add 1 ¾ C chopped dates dredged lightly with flour and 1 C chopped walnuts or macadamia nut bits. Grease 9″ × 13″ shallow pan, spread ½″ deep, and bake in 350–375 F oven for 30 minutes. Cut in bars while hot, roll in confectionary sugar, cool and store in containers. Yield: about 24.

Oatmeal Cookies

Cream ¼ lb. soft butter with 1 C sugar. Add 1 beaten egg, 2 T flour and 1 t baking powder sifted together and 1 C quick oatmeal and 1 t vanilla. Add nuts if desired—½ C. Grease cookie sheet, sprinkle with flour. Drop 1 t full at a time and leave room for spreading. Bake in 325 F oven for 10–12 minutes. Wait a few minutes to cool but before cookies harden, loosen and remove with spatula to cooling rack. These are very lacy and delicate.

Russian Tea Cakes

Mix 1 C soft butter, ½ C powdered sugar, 2¼ C flour and ¼ t soda sifted together. Add 1 t vanilla and ¾ C chopped nuts. Mix well, form into balls, bake at 400 F for 14–17 minutes. While hot, roll in icing sugar and cool. When cold roll again in icing sugar. Delicious! Yield: 60–70.

Potato Cake

BETTY (MRS. LUKE) HEBERT has lived at Kahuku plantation for many years and still swears by this old homemade cake.

Cream together ½ C soft butter and 2 C sugar. Add 1 C mashed potatoes (hot or cold). Add 4 well-beaten eggs and 2 C flour sifted together with 2 t baking powder, ½ C ground chocolate, 1 t cinnamon, 1 t mace, ¼ t cloves alternately with ½ C milk. When well blended add 1 C chopped walnuts. Bake at 350 for 45 minutes in well greased loaf pan or two round cake pans.

Chocolate Morsel Dessert

LEILA (MRS. JAMES F.) MORGAN, JR. prefaced this recipe with a note: "See how easy!." And oh . . . so delicious!

Combine 1 6 oz. pkg. semi-sweet chocolate morsels, 1 T instant coffee, 2 T sugar and 2 T water in top of double boiler, stir to blend, cool. Add 3 egg yolks one at a time, beating after each. Stir in 1 t vanilla and few grains of salt. Beat egg whites stiff, fold in. Crumble vanilla wafers on bottom of refrigerator tray, pour mixture over it. Chill several hours or overnight. Serve with whipped cream.

Bartlett Pears in Wine

STEPHEN COOKE makes this dessert when fresh Bartlett pears flood the market, and it is outstandingly different.

Have 6 green Bartlett pears, the greener and harder the better. Peel skin with potato peeler, quarter lengthwise and remove seeds and strings. Add these to a pot containing: ½ C water, 1½ C sugar, 2 heaping T cinnamon, 1 quart of red Burgundy and pinch of salt. (Throw in the peelings when cooking for more pectin, but remove when done.) Bring this to a boil, turn heat to simmer about 10 minutes, lift pears out with slotted spoon, lay in rows on shallow baking pan and set aside to cool. Simmer juice down to two-thirds, pour over pears and chill for at least four hours. Serve with whipped cream or ice cream.

Coco Cake

MURIEL (MRS. WALTER E.) FLANDERS always remembers her grandmother, "Omama" MacFarlane (MRS. F. W.), making this chocolate cake for all the children. The recipe is written in her handwriting on note paper with the heading, AHUIMANU, the family ranch home in the valley behind Kahaluu.

¾ C shortening, 1½ C sugar, 1 ¾ C flour, ¾ C sour milk or buttermilk, ½ C coarsely cut up nuts (toasted), ½ t baking powder, ½ t soda, ½ t salt, ¾ t nutmeg, 1 t cinnamon, 1 T cocoa, 3 eggs, 1 t vanilla, 1 t lemon extract. Cream the shortening and add sugar gradually. Cream thoroughly. Blend in the 3 well-beaten eggs. Sift flour once before measuring. Sift the flour, baking powder, soda, salt, spices, and cocoa all together and add to the creamed mixture alternately with the sour milk. Stir in the flavoring and nuts. Then pour out into well-greased and floured layer cake pans. Bake for 30 minutes in a moderate oven (350 F) then add icing.

Icing: Cream 6 T butter and blend in yolk of 1 egg. Sift 3 C confectioners sugar, 1½ t cocoa, and 1 t cinnamon all together then add to creamed mixture alternately with 1½ T hot coffee. Beat until smooth. If necessary add a few more drops of coffee until the icing spreads easily.

Shortbread Cookies

MURIEL (MRS. WALTER E.) FLANDERS says she's not a cookie-maker, but that these are absolutely foolproof!

Cream 1 C butter or margarine with ¾ C sugar until fluffy. Add 1 egg, unbeaten, 1 t vanilla, and 2½ C flour sifted together with ½ t baking powder, ⅛ t salt. Mix well and drop on ungreased cookie tin and press flat with hand. Bake in 400 F oven for 10–12 minutes.

Mrs. Kopke's Plum Pudding

MARTHA (MRS. JAMES M.) GREENWELL has vivid memories of great family Christmas dinners at Grandma Kopke's (Mrs. Ernst) home. The blazing plum pudding was the star attraction not only because Grandma Kopke made it herself from a recipe she

brought from Australia but because she gave the greatest joy to the young children when they found the ring, dime, thimble or other trinkets in the pudding. (Why, oh why, has this exciting childhood tradition been lost and forgotten in this practical age?)

This was made about a month before Christmas. 1¼ lb. stale bread crumbs; 1 lb. seedless raisins; 1 lb. currants; 1 lb. brown sugar; 1 lb. beef suet, chopped fine; ½ lb. candied peel mix; 12 eggs; ½ T each nutmeg, ginger, cloves, allspice, cinnamon; ½ t salt and 1 tumbler brandy (8 oz.? 16 oz.? how big were the tumblers in those days?) Mix all together well. Divide the boiled and sterilized money and trinkets in evenly. Put in plum pudding tins, tightly seal, and steam for 3 hours. One week later steam 1 hour. Then steam 1 hour before serving. Pour brandy over, light, and bring flaming to the table. Hard sauce or vanilla ice cream is served with this—or both.

Pineapple Ice Box Cake

MARTHA (MRS. JAMES M.) GREENWELL remembers coming home from school to find a little leftover dessert from her mother's luncheons (Mrs. Sherwood Lowrey). "This one was my favorite because it wasn't as rich in calories as the other whip cream varieties!"

You need a spring mold (can still be bought in any hardware store) and 3 doz. lady fingers primarily.

PART I: 1 large C crushed pineapple, drained; 2 T orange or lemon juice; 4 T cornstarch, moistened; 4 egg yolks beaten; ½ C sugar; ¼ C pineapple juice. Put pineapple, juice, and sugar in double boiler. When hot add cornstarch and cook until transparent. Add beaten egg yolks and cook quickly for only 1 or 2 minutes. Remove from fire and let mixture cool.

PART II: Cream well ¾ C butter and 1 C powdered sugar. Add pinch of salt, ½ C finely chopped walnuts, and 1 t vanilla. Add part I to part II and fold in well-beaten egg whites to which you must add 2 T powdered sugar. Line bottom of spring mold with split lady fingers, and line sides, adding mixture to fill and hold. Refrigerate for 24 hours. Serve with a dab of whipped cream.

Haupia Cake

IRMGARD (MRS. NANE) ALULI is a member of the well-known Farden family from Maui. Coming from a musically inclined family, it is only natural that she has played a guitar or ukulele all her life and her harmonizing at beach picnics still sounds the same today as it did many, many years ago. She has composed many Island tunes and is a true child of Hawaii. This recipe was given to Irmgard by friends.

Cream ½ lb. butter with 1 ¾ C sugar until fluffy. Add 4 beaten eggs then 3 C flour sifted with 6 t baking powder, 1 level t baking soda, and pinch of salt alternately with 1 C orange passion juice (frozen, undiluted). Bake at 350 F oven in two layer pans for 30–35 mins.

For frosting make *haupia* but cut down on cornstarch so as to make it spreading instead of cutting consistency. Put between layers and over top. Let this settle then add a frosting of either whipped cream flavored with vanilla or a frothy white sugar icing. Chill and serve cold.

HAUPIA: Bring to boil 2 C thawed frozen coconut milk. Add slowly ½ C sugar, ¼ t salt, 3 T cornstarch dissolved in ½ C cold water. Stir constantly until it thickens. You can tell when it's done when it is clear and the mixture coats the spoon. Cool and add vanilla.

Cheese Cake

ALEXANDRA (MRS. J. MARK) WEBSTER, daughter of a *kamaaina* family, and her husband are popular young members of a sugar plantation community on the big island of Hawaii. Plantation life during the week means hard work and hours that begin long before the average businessman starts his day. Saturday is the night to entertain and guests come from long distances and other plantations. "So," says "Alex." "You just don't have a cocktail party! Hearty *pupus*, wash tubs filled with ice and beer, meaty casseroles, French bread, tossed salads, coffee, and a rich dessert are a must—and plenty of it all!'' Her favorite dessert recipe could only be for the young whose energy fends off the poundage.

CRUST: 1¼ C crushed graham crackers, 4 T ground almonds or walnuts, 2 T sugar, 1 t grated lemon peel, ½ C melted butter.

FILLING: 1¼ lbs. soft cream cheese, 1 C sugar, 1 t vanilla, 3 t lemon juice, 1 t lemon rind and 4 eggs.

TOPPING: 1 pt. ice-cold sour cream, ½ C sugar, ½ t vanilla.

1. Combine crumbs, nuts, sugar, lemon peel. Stir in butter until thoroughly blended. Press mixture firmly against bottom of 9″ spring form. Bake in 350 F oven for 10 mins.

2. In large bowl of mixer, beat cheese until creamy. At medium speed add sugar gradually, then vanilla, lemon juice, and rind and blend well. Add eggs, 1 at a time and beat at medium speed for 10 mins. until fluffy. Pour into pan. Bake at 250 oven for 35 mins. Turn off heat and cool for 30 mins. in oven with door open.

3. Combine sour cream, sugar and vanilla and whip for 10 mins. until foamy, spoon over top of cake. Bake in 250 oven for 10 mins. Sprinkle with cinnamon. Cool. Refrigerate for 2 hrs. before serving. You may freeze it and on the serving day remove from spring pan and thaw in refrigerator for 4 or 5 hrs. Provides 16–18 servings.

MISCELLANY

Chili Pepper Water

PEGGY MAY (MRS. ROBERT) HUNTER always keeps a bottle of chili pepper water available in the icebox. Divine fresh substitute for Tabasco sauce. She half fills a silver and crystal bitters bottle with washed and stemmed red chili peppers and adds gin for liquid. The popular recipe uses a ketsup bottle! Fill the bottle three quarters full of water, empty into pot, add pinch of Hawaiian salt, and when it bubbles turn off the fire and throw in a handful of firm red chili peppers. A few small cloves of garlic are optional. Cool and keep refrigerated . . . the longer it stands the hotter the fire!

Seaweed (Limu)

It's great sport diving for *limu* or wading out to exposed reefs at low tide and braving the pounding waves to pick it; devilish to clean; but oh so *ono* and good for you—iron and iodine. In the olden days the Hawaiians had no refrigeration, so they picked, cleaned and ate the *limu* the same day. Today you may store bottled *limu* in the refrig for quite a while. After picking *maneoneo* (Japanese seaweed or *ogo*), wash and clean in two tubs of water, picking off all tiny rocks, roots, and other foreign *limu*. It takes several "pickings" and changes of water to clean the *limu* properly.

To cook: drop the *limu* into boiling water for barely two minutes—it will turn a lighter color. Drain in colander, put in bowl, add Hawaiian salt and vinegar to taste, chopped tomatoes, onions, and chili pepper are optional. Keep in tightly covered jars in the refrig.

Limu kohu is a lovely sight to behold in the water—beds of waving featherylike stems. Being delicate it is harder to clean the fragile stems of grit, other weeds and minute debris. When well cleaned and rinsed, chop up and add some Hawaiian salt to taste. Set aside in frig for one day. Squeeze out liquid, roll into a ball and bottle. Keep in tightly covered jar in refrig. Some people freeze *limu*, but old-timers will tell you this makes the *limu* dry and lose all its strength when thawed.

Fresh Accent

At their beach home on Hawaii the Lloyd

Sextons use the large, green Tahitian *hau* tree leaves as place mats at dinner, and with gay flowered paper napkins it sets a happy informal mood. Of course, Tahitian *hau* leaves aren't available to everyone, but if you use your eyes and imagination you can find substitutes!

Old Time Recipes

"Steve" (Mrs. Allen C.) Wilcox through her journalistic career has become immersed in Hawaiiana and Island lore. She found these two recipes in the "Ladies Society of Central Union Church Cook Book" published in 1888. The first recipe absolutely intrigued her to the point of sharing!

Soup de Corbeaux

Contributed by Mr. A. Marques

Clean two young mynah birds and roast them in butter adding salt when nearly cooked. Let them get cold, cut them up and pound them—flesh and bones—in a mortar until you obtain a kind of paste which you mix up with warm water or broth. Flavor to taste and keep it hot in "boiu maise" (a dish of boiling water) until ready for use. Then pass it through a fine sieve and throw it on slices of bread toasted, or better **still**, fried in butter.

Pop Robin

Contributed by Miss Fidelia Lyons
1 qt. sweet milk put over the fire. When it comes to a boil stir in 1 egg beaten together with 2 spoonfuls of flour and a little milk and a little salt. Serve hot. A simple dish for tea. (A rare understatement!)
HELEN (MRS. ALAN S.) DAVIS adds a pretty new twist to ridding closets of bugs! Buy a firm medium-size apple and poke in cloves to cover *completely*. Tie narrow velvet ribbon around and tie bow at stem end. Keep in place by sticking common pins through small pearls. These make particularly good presents at Christmas. Strangely enough these keep for years!

Ginger

The fragrant white or yellow ginger blossom is considered dear and special by most Islanders. IRMGARD (MRS. NANE) ALULI has a special way of treating them for longer and hardier life. Cut the stalk and crush the ends so it can absorb the water more readily and plunge in deep water. Pour water into the blossom stalk so the flowers themselves have lots to drink. Then cut and shape the leaves or strip away any large ones so that the heads of flowers are featured and not hidden in the bouquet. Daily remove dead flowers and add more water to stalks and blossom heads.

Puolo

IRMGARD ALULI still uses this old-fashioned Island way of wrapping *leis* to take to dear friends for special occasions. She cuts a whole *ti* leaf head, leaving about 12″ of stalk. Rinse off and turn the stalk upside down so the leaves spread like an umbrella. Then loosely lay the woven or strung *leis* (fern, rose, ginger, ilima) around the stalk, grab up the leaves from the sides, and bring up over the stalk to form round bundle. Hold securely and tie with ribbed *ti* leaves which have been joined together. If this is too difficult, tie securely with florist twine to hold, then wrap *ti* leaves around to form "ribbon and bow" and decorate with flowers.

For a lighter *puolo* rinse a dozen or more long green *ti* leaves. Grab stem ends together and bind at lower end of stem nearest leaf. Wrap *lei* around this, gather up the leaves around the *lei* so that the shiny side stands outside, and form bundle. Secure top of the leaves around the mid stem with wire or *ti* leaves and add bow and flowers.

Irmgard usually picks flowers (anthuriums, pink shell and red ginger, bird of paradise or ferns) from the garden for her *malihini* friends and delivers them in her own "box." Take two young banana leaves and lay them flat end to end, place colored or green *ti* leaves on top of this with stems overlapping and then lay the flowers and ferns end to end on this. Roll banana leaves over to close, leaving the ends open. Join two *ti* leaves to bind and tie center. Decorate top with flowers or *ti* leaf bow. It is a joyful gift in truly Hawaiian fashion, but remember to remind them that banana stains.

Another Irmgard innovation: for a Hawaiian luncheon with no silverware she strips the mid rib of the coconut leaves and scrapes it well with a knife to smoothen and breaks them into about 4″ lengths. Then she threads Island fruits on this, places them in shallow dish, pours any Island fruit juice over, and serves this as the first course!

Niu Haohao

Irmgard remembers her mother ANNIE (MRS. SHAW) FARDEN entertaining at tea in Lahaina, Maui. The day before, the boys would shimmy up the trees to strip them of all the young nuts, husk them, crack and pour the water into a large container and add the scooped out tender meat in small pieces. This was refrigerated overnight. The day of the tea she served this very, very cold (no ice) in a large punchbowl with punch cups. For other occasions Mrs. Farden added a bit of gin. And the song goes: "*He ono ka wai o ka niu haohao, haohao*—delicious is the water of the young coconut with soft meat."

Boiled Water

And when all else fails, says MRS. ALICE KAMOKILA CAMPBELL—1. Put water in pot. 2. Put pot on stove and bring to boil. 3. Remove from stove. The *best boiled water* you've ever tasted!!!

CHRONOLOGY

JANUARY 1st: big day for the Japanese, bamboo in front doors, rising at dawn, preparation and eating of great feasts, and a general tradition of family spirit and fellowship for the coming new year.

FEBRUARY: Chinese new year time generally (date is set by the lunar calendar)—Kung Hee Fat Choy—a year of an animal—fire crackers galore, tangerines, cakes, and lots of tradition. The lovely, delicate narcissus flower blooms and a queen is crowned from among the Chinese beauties.

MARCH 3rd: Japanese girl's day, gifts of dolls. March 26th: Hawaiian Holiday honoring the birthday of the late Prince Kuhio, delegate to Congress, who did so much for his fellow Hawaiians.

APRIL: Battle of Nuuanu in which Kamehameha I engaged the Oahuans in battle and pushed them over the pali and crowned himself King of the Hawaiian chain.

MAY 1st: Lei Day in Hawaii! Everybody wears a lei, a queen holds court, a lei contest out of the ordinary, and photographers go wild. May 5th: Japanese Boys' Day—large red paper carp fly over housetops to proclaim the number of lads in the household.

JUNE 11th: Hawaiian Holiday honoring the birthday of King Kamehameha I, the great warrior. Spectacular morning parade with lovely *pa-u* riders (women riding side saddle with flowing silken riding habits), floral floats, bands, crack military units, and general excitement and celebrating.

JULY 7, 1898: Annexation day—down came Hawaiian flag and up went "Old Glory"—sad day for old Hawaiians.

AUGUST 21, 1959: Hawaii sheds territorial status and becomes 50th state.

SEPTEMBER: School as usual.

OCTOBER: Aloha Week celebrated. Everyone wears Hawaiian garb, lots of special attractions for tourist and residents alike.

NOVEMBER 16, 1836: the gay King Kalakaua born.

DECEMBER 7, 1941: "Remember Pearl Harbor." World War II.

GLOSSARY

ahi	Hawaiian tuna fish	*hale*	house
alani awa-awa	calmondin orange	*haupia*	coconut pudding
aumakua	personal god	*holoku*	loosely fitted dress with train
awa	root of shrub from which strong brew is made	*hookupu*	special gift

hula	Hawaiian dance	*mele*	chant
imu	underground oven	*nei*	this
inamona	relish made from kukui nut	*ni'au*	mid-rib of coconut leaf
kahi	scrape	*okolehao*	liquor made from ti root
kalua	bake in underground oven	*ola*	life
kanaka	Hawaiian being	*ono*	delicious
kamaaina	born of the Islands	*opakapaka*	sweet Hawaiian fish
keiki o ka aina	child of the land	*opihis*	limpet
kiawe	algaroba tree	*pa'a kai*	salt
kukui	candlenut tree	*palapalai*	fern
kuu home	home sweet home	*paniolo*	Hawaiian cowboy
lauhala	pandanus leaf	*pau*	finished
laulau	package of pork and luau leaves wrapped in ti leaves	*Pele*	Hawaiian goddess of fire
		pipi	beef
lawai	native fern	*pipikaula*	jerk beef
leis	garlands	*poi*	Hawaiian staff of life—made from taro
lilikoi	purple water lemon		
limu	seaweed	*pupu*	hors d'oeuvre
lomi	massage, squeeze or crush	*tabu*	forbidden
luau	native feast	*tapa*	material made from bark
luau leaves	green leaves of taro plant	*taro*	tuberous root
mahalo	thank you	*ti*	plant with large green leaf
maile	fragrant vine; leis made from leaves	*ulu*	breadfruit
		ulua	Hawaiian jack fish
malihini	newcomer to Hawaii	*hibachi*	small Japanese grill
malo	loin cloth	*mama-san*	title of respect
maneo	itchy, irritating	*tempura*	fried in batter
mauka	toward the mountains		

WHO'S WHO

Peasons Whose Names Appear in This Book

Aluli, Irmgard (Mrs. Nane) 95, 98
Apo, Lambert, 51, 79, 90
Armitage, Yvonne (Mrs. John) 40
Bachman, Adel (Mrs. Lyle) 51, 56
Bartow, Mary, 9
Bazore, Katherine, 9
Bisho, Bella, 13
Blythe, Peggy (Mrs. Douglas) 78
Bowen, Mrs. Alice Spalding, 88
Broadbent, Beth (Mrs. Frank W.) 58
Bryan, Shada (Mrs. Ed.) 21, 51, 66, 81
Campbell, Mrs. Alice Kamokila, 99
Carter, Catharine (Mrs. Reginald H.) 29, 36, 44, 92
Catton, Mrs. Robert A., 83
Chang, Bob, 30
Chillingsworth, Ann (Mrs. Charles) 35
Cooke, Mr. & Mrs. George, 15
Cooke, Stephen, 43, 59
Davis, Helen (Mrs. Alan S.) 98
de Paula Marin, Don Francisco, 10
Derby, Dora (Mrs. Stephen A.) 20, 50, 90
Dillingham, Ben F., 21
Dillingham, Mrs. Walter F., 14, 21, 42, 55, 56, 57

Evans, Cleo (Mrs. Robert) 21, 57
Farden, Annie (Mrs. Shaw) 99
Flanders, Muriel (Mrs. Walter E.) 21, 60, 67, 94
Flanders, Walter, 45
Forster, Mame, 30
Frost, Adeline Hose, 5
Greenwell, Martha (Mrs. James M.) 94
Hebert, Betty (Mrs. Luke) 92
Holmes, Ohris, 15
Hunter, Peggy May (Mrs. Robert) 22, 26
Irwin, Miss, 10
Judd, L. McCully, Jr., 55
Judd, Martha (Mrs. J. Robert) 28, 35
Judd, Ruthie (Mrs. L. McCully, Jr.) 42, 79, 92
Kai, Ernest K., 53
Kalakaua, King, 11
Kamehameha I, 10
Kawananakoa, Princess David, 11, 15
Kimball, Mrs. Clifford H. 30
Kopke, Mrs. Ernst, 94
Lewis, Dudley, 43
Lloyd, Miss Healani, 21, 30, 31
Lyons, Miss Fidelia, 98

Marques, Mr. A., 97
Mendonca, Mrs. Lucy, 53
Miller, Carey D., 9
Miller, Ollie (Mrs. R. L.) 36, 40, 87
Moir, Mae (Mrs. Goodale) 82, 91
Morgan, Leila (Mrs. James F.) 93
Palma, Julie (Mrs. Joseph), 88
Pang, Dolly (Mrs. Herbert G.) 52
Parer, Ekrnest, 11
Patton, General, 14
Peterson, Leinani (Mrs. E. B.) 34, 42, 54
Richert, "Tetta" (Mrs. Thomas) 36, 77, 87
Robinson, Charles, 79, 80
Ross, "Baby" May (Mrs. Alexander) 89
Sexton, Mr. & Mrs. Lloyd, 97
Sloggett, Diane (Mrs. Arthur C.) 58

Sutherland, "Sis" (Mrs. Ross) 34
Thompson, Mrs. Frank, 34, 79
Throckmorton, Sybil (Mrs. Russel C.) 41, 58
Wales, Prince of, 12
Walker, Jack (Mr. John C.) 29, 54, 66, 82, 89
Walker, Mrs. John S., 89
Webster, Alexandra (Mrs. J. Mark) 95
Wilcox, "Steve" (Mrs. Allen C.) 97
Wilder, Kinau, 56, 78
Wilder, Sarah, 40, 52, 66, 89
Williams, Jimmy, 11
Windsor, Duke of, 12
Yardley, Paul, 9

INDEX

abalone, 18
    pork-abalone soup (pake), 28
Ajinomoto, 16
Alexander Young Hotel, 14
alligator pears, see avocados
aloe, 16
angel food cake, 87
apple, mountain, 68
aspic, tomato salad, 34
avacados, 71

avacados (continued)
dip, 18
dressing for, 34
salad, 33, 34
sandwich, 28
soup, cold, 28
soup, iced, 39
bacon
chutney-bacon spread, 31
cream cheese-bacon spread, 21

bananas, 69
  au rum, 84
  baked, 64
    Sarah wilder's, 66
    with coconut cream, 85
  cake, 84
  fried, 64
  glazed, 64
  marmalade, 76
  muffins, 89
  peanut butter-banana sandwich, 28
  salad, 33
bean thread (long rice)
  Naka's, 60
  with chicken, 49
beef
  and tomatoes, ~~45~~ 55
  corned, sandwich spread, 28
  jerky, 46, 47
  Stroganoff, with coconut, 51
  terriyaki sticks, 19
beet soup, chilled, 28
berries, ohelo, 68
beverages, 22–25
biscuits, taro, 62
bonito, baked (aku), 40
boulabaisse, 43
breadfruit, 65, 69
  chips, 21
bread, mango, 85
cabbage
  cole slaw, 32
  red, 67
cakes
  angel food, 87
  banana, 84

cheese, 95
  coco, 93
  haupia, 95
  passion fruit, 87
  pineapple ice box, 94
  pineapple upside-down, 90
  potato, 92
  taro, 21, 62, 66
calamondin, 72
  jam, 78
  preserve, 80
candy, coconut, 77
carambola, 71
carissa, 72
  jelly, 76
carrots, dilled, 81
caterers, 17
cheese cake, 95
cheese-chutney spread, 18
cherries, Surinam, 71
  jelly, 76, 78
  sauce, 81
cherry tomatoes with salmon, 19
chicken
  broiled, baked, or barbecued, 58
  coconut chicken, 49
  lei moni, 58
  long rice with chicken, 49
  luau, 58
  oriental, 49
  poulet truffe a l'Armagnac, 59
  sandwich spread, 31
  soup (jook), 26
  with papaya, 50
  with spinach and coconut, 58
chili pepper water, 96

Chinese
  five spices, 17
  fotune cookies, 86
  jook (soup), 26
  orange marmalade, 83
  peas, 65
  preserved candy, 86
  rice puffs, 86
  spare ribs, 60
  tongue, 51
chips, breadfruit, 21
chocolate cake (coco), 93
chocolate morsel dessert, 93
chook (soup), 26
chops, pork, 56
chop suey, 49
chowder
  boulabaisse, 43
  fish, 26, 28, 29, 41
chronology, 99–100
chutney
  bacon-chutney spread, 31
  mango, 74, 78, 79
  papaya, 83
  tamarind-mango, 82
  toast rounds, 21
clove-apple bug repellent, 98
coconut, 69
  candy, 77
  cream, with baked bananas, 85
  dessert, 85
  milk, 77
    frozen, 17
    haupia, 90
  shortbread cookies, 86
  with beef Stroganoff, 51

  with chicken, 49
  with chicken and spinach, 58
  with spinach, 64
cocktail parties, 17
cole slaw, 32
coffee, 24
  iced, 24
  vodka-coffee-vanilla sauce, 23
compote flambé, 89
compote pineapple, 86
cookies
  coconut shortbread, 86
  date bars, 92
  fortune, 86
  oatmeal, 92
  Russian tea cakes, 92
  shortbread, 94
corned beef, 61
  spread, 28
corn soup, cream of, 29
cream puffs, 88
cream, sour, with fish, 40
crabmeat, creamed, with macaroni, 42
cucumber
  salad, Japanese, 33
  salad, pineapple, 34
  sandwich, open-face, 30
curry
  dip, 18
  fool-proof, 56
  Hawaiian, 56, 57
  lamb, 48
  sauce, 57
daquiri, 23
date bars, 92
Day, C. J., Market, 10

desserts, 84–96
dips
  avacado, 18
  curry, 18
dolphin (mahimahi)
  broiled, 43
  fried, 44
dressing
  French, 34
  green goddess, 36
  salad, 34
    for avacados, 34
  "Tetta's", 36
  vinaigrette, 36
drinks, 22–25
egg nog, 25
eggs
  eggnog, 25
  Florentine, 36
  scrambled with tomatoes, 67
    with tuna fish, 45
  stuffed, 21
figs, 68
  spiced, 79
fish, 19–20, 26–29, 37–45
  and macaroni (fish dish), 41
  baked, 39
  bonito, baked (aku), 40
  boulabaisse, 43
  broiled, 38
    mahimahi, 43
  chowder, 12, 26, 28, 29, 41
  crab, creamed, with macaroni, 42
  fried, 38, 40
    mahimahi, 44
  Hawaiian names, 38

  in sour cream, 40
  kedgeree, 44
  mahimahi
    broiled, 43
    fried, 44
  pudding, 42
  raw, 19, 20
  salmon, lomi, 39, 41
  salmon mousse, 44
  soup, 27
  steamed, 38
  tuna, baked (ahi), 40
Five Islands Gin, 14
five spices, Chinese, 17
Five Ulcers (beverage), 14
flambé compote, 89
Florentine eggs, 36
Ford Island, 14
French dressing, 34
fruits and preserves, 68–84. *See* names of
  specific fruits.
garlic, 16
gelatin
  guava, 90, 91
  pineapple salad, 33
ginger
  blossoms, 98
  root, 16
  sandwiches, 30
  sauce, 88
glossary, 100–101
grapefruit, 72
grape pie, 87
grapes, Isabella, 68
  spiced, 83
guava, 70

gelatin, 90, 91
jam, 75, 78
jelly, 74
mousse, 91
pulp, freezing of, 90
shells, cooked, 91
strawberry, 71
Halekulani Hotel, 30
hamburger, gourmet, 59
hash, wine, 54
haupia, 90
cake, 95
Hawaii Visitor's Bureau, 15
hors d'oeuvres, 17–22
jam, *see also* jelly; marmalade
calamondin, 78
guava, 75, 78
pineapple, 76
poha, 76
Japanese
cucumber salad, 33
tuna and egg, 45
Java plums, 68
jelly, *see also* jam; marmalade
bag, 16
carissa, 76
guava, 74
mango, 83
passion fruit, 76
pepper pot, 79
seagrape, 73
surinam cherry, 76, 78
jerky beef, 46–47
jook (soup), 26
Kahala Beach, 14
Kalua pig platter, 18

Kapiolani Park, 14
Kedgeree, 44
kukui not, 79
kuu home kalua, 23
lamb
curry, 48
leg of, 48, 55
leg of, butterfly, 54
leis, wrapping, 98
lemon, water, 71
Liberty House, 10
limes, 72
pie, 92
long rice
Naka's, 60
with chicken, 49
lotus root pupu, 12
luau leaves, 63
lychees, 72
in kirsch, 86
mango-lychee dessert, 88
salad, 34
stuffed, 21
macadamia nuts, 20
cheese spread, 31
macaroni
fish dish, 41
with creamed crab, 42
mai tai (beverage), 23
mango, 69
bread, 85
champagned, 88
chutney, 74, 78, 79
jelly, 83
lychee-mango dessert, 88
pickled, 73

mango (*continued*)
  pickled (*continued*)
    sweet, 83
  pie, 85
  salad, 34
  sauce, 86
  tamarind-mango chutney, 82
marmalade, *see also* jam; jelly
  banana, 76
  orange, 83
  pineapple-papaya, 75
  pudding, 89
  guava-pineapple, 75
Maui (island), 17
meats, *see* bacon; beef; chicken; chops;
  chop suey; corned beef; hamburger;
  lamb; pork; spare ribs; stew; tongue;
  tripe; turkey; venison
Metropolitan Meat Market, 10
milk, coconut, 77
  frozen, 17
minted pineapple, 86
mint sherbet, 55
miscellany, 96–99
miso soup, 27
Molokai, 15
mountain apples, 68
mousse
  guava, 91
  salmon, 44
  soursop, 85
muffins, banana, 89
mulberries, 68
mulligatawny soup, 30
mynah birds, roasted, 97
niu haohao, 99

nuts
  kukui, 79
  macadamia, 20
    sandwich spread, 31
  peanuts, 20
oatmeal cookies, 92
ohelo berries, 68
okolehao, 22, 24
onions, 16
  pickled, 82
  pie, 67
  purple, marinated, 21
  soup, 29
  tomato-onion salad, 35
oranges
  kona, 72
  marmalade, 83
ox tail soup, 27
pake (pork-abalone soup), 28
papaya, 70
  baked, 65
  chicken in papaya, 50
  chutney, 83
  pickle, sweet, 83
  pineapple-papaya marmalade, 75
parsley tempura, 66
passion fruit, 71
  cake, 87
  jelly, 76
peanut butter-banana sandwich, 28
Pearl Harbor, 14
pears, bartlett, in wine, 93
peas
  Chinese, 65
  split, soup, 29
pelum, 16

pepper pot jelly, 79
pickles
   mango, 73
     sweet, 83
   mixed 81
   onion, 82
   papaya, 83
   pineapple, 76, 80, 81
pies
   grape, 87
   lime, 92
   mango, 85
   onion, 67
   pumpkin, 87
Pietra, La, 14
pineapple
   cake, ice box, 94
   cake, upside-down, 90
   canned, 17
   compote, 86
   gelatin salad, 33
   guava-pineapple marmalade, 75
   jam, 76
   minted, 86
   papaya-pineapple marmalade, 75
   pickled, 76, 80, 81
   salad, 33, 34
plums, 71
   Java, 68
   pudding, 94
pohas, 69
   jam, 76
poi, 62–63
   cocktail, 24
pork, *see also* bacon
   chops, 56

giant laulaus, 46
kalua pig platter, 18
oven kalua, 46
pake (soup), 28
Portuguese holiday, 53
Portuguese
   holiday pork, 53
   sausage, 21
potato
   cake, 92
   salad, 32, 35
preserves, 73
   calamondin, 72
pudding
   fish, 42
   marmalade, 89
   plum, 94
puffs
   cream, 88
   rice, 86
   taro, 62
pumpkin pie, 87
punch, fruit, 25
punk, 16
pupus, 17–22
Queen's Surf, 15
rice, 64
   fried, 64
rice, long
   Naka's, 60
   with chicken, 49
rock salt, 16
Royal Hawaiian Hotel, 14, 15
Russian tea cakes, 92
saké, 24
salads, 31–36

salads (*continued*)
avacado, 34
  stuffed, 33
banana, 33
cole slaw, 32
combination, 34
cucumber, Japanese, 33
cucumber-pineapple, 34
dressing, 34
  for avacados, 34
  green goddess, 36
  "Tetta's", 36
lychee, 34
mango, 34
pineapple, 33
  gelatin, 33
potato, 32, 35
salmon
  lomi, 39, 41
  mousse, 44
  with cherry tomatoes, 19
salt, rock, Hawaiian, 16
sandwiches, 28, 30–31
avacado, 28
banana-peanut butter, 28
chicken, 31
chutney-bacon, 31
corned beef, 28
cucumber open face, 30
ginger, 30
luncheon meat, 31
shrimp, 31
tuna, 28
sashimi, 19, 20
sauces
chili pepper water, 96

curry, 57
for fried fish, 40
ginger, 88
kuu home kualua (vodka-coffee-vanilla), 23
mango, 86
soy, 16, 55
  basic, 18
  for steaks, 56
steak, 54
surinam cherry, 81
tartar, 31
sausage, Portuguese, 21
scorpions (beverage), 22, 23
seagrape, 73
jelly, 78
seaweed, 96
sherbet
mint, 55
soursop, 85
shortbread cookies, 94
coconut, 86
shrimp
sandwich spread, 31
tempura, 20
soup, 26–31, *see also* chowder
avacado, cold, 28
avacado, iced, 30
beet, chilled, 28
corn, cream of, 29
fish, 27
jook or chook (fowl), 26
miso, 27
mulligatawny, 30
onion, 29
ox tail, 27

pake (pork-abalone), 28
spinach, cream, 29
split pea, 29
sour cream with fish, 40
soursop, 71
    mousse, 85
    sherbet, 85
soy beans, 66
soy sauce, 16, 18
    basic, 18
    for steaks, 56
    with leg of lamb, 55
spare ribs, 51
    Cantonese, 60
    ewa beef riblets, 52
    sweet sour, 52
spinach
    cream soup, 29
    with chicken, 58
    with coconut, 65 64
split pea soup, 29
spreads
    bacon-cheese, 21
    chicken, 31
    chutney-bacon, 31
    corned beef, 28
    luncheon meat, 31
    shrimp, 31
steak sauce, 54
stew
    Hawaiian, 53
        bibi, 50
        with luau, 47
    kanaka, 51
strawberry guavas, 71
sugar, raw, 17

suicide (beverage), 23
surinam cherries, 71
    jelly, 76, 78
    sauce, 87
sweet-sour spare ribs, 52
syrup, tamarind, 82
table decor, 12
Tahitian fish, raw,
tamarind, 68
    mango-tamarind chutney, 82
    syrup, 82
tangarines, 72
taro
    biscuits, 62
    cakes, 21, 62, 66
    puffs, 62
tea, iced, 24, 25
tempura
    parsley, 66
    shrimp, 20
terriyaki
    meat, 51, 60
    sauce, 48, 49
    sticks, 19
ti leaf wrapping for leis, 98
toast, chutney, 21
tomatoes
    and beef, 55
    aspic salad, 34
    onion-tomato salad, 35
    with scrambled eggs, 67
tomatoes, cherry, with salmon, 19
tongue
    Chinese style, 51
    smoked, 52
tripe, hale ola, 52

tuna fish
    baked (ahi), 40
    sandwich, 28
    with scrambled eggs, 45
turkey salad, 33
upside-down cake, pineapple, 90
vanilla-vodka-coffee sauce, 23
vegetables, 61–67. *See* names of specific
    vegetables
venison, 47
vinaigrette dressing, 36
vodka-coffee-vanilla sauce, 23

Waialae Golf Club, 14
Waiohai Hotel, 30
water, boiled, 99
water lemon, 71
watercress, 65
watermelon, 71
    bowl, 89
    dessert, 91
who's who, 102
wine
    hash, 54
    with bartlett pears, 93
won ton, 19

Japanese Embassy

Dinner

To His Majesty the King,

Staff Officers, Ministers of the Crown and Diplomatic Corps,

January 10th, 1870.

SOUPS.

Green Turtle Soup,　　　Tomato Soup.

FISH.

Poison Bouillie,　　　Poison en Cassarole,

Poison en Cadina,　　　Pieche Mollier,

Crabs en Farcie.

ROASTS.

Boned Turkey,　　　Roast Goose,

Boiled Turkey, oyster sauce,　　Raised Turtle Pie,

Boiled Ham.

VEGETABLES.

Green Peas,　　Boiled Potatoes,　　Mashed Potatoes,

Turnips,　　Rice Croquets.

ENTREES.

Canard Sauvage aux olives,　　Bras a la Tortue,

Shrimp Curry,　　Plover,　　Cotelletts de Tortue.

Pigeons with mushrooms,

Salads, Plain and Chicken.

DESSERT.

English Pudding,　　Gipsey Pudding,　　Wine Jellies,

Strawberries and Ice Cream,　　　Fruit Cakes,

Sponge Cakes,　　Assorted small Cakes.

Nuts,　　Fruits,　　Coffee,　　Tea and Liquors,

WINES.

Sherry, Hock, Claret, Champagne, Burgundy, Sparkling Hock.